DESIGN AND ANALYSIS OF HUMAN RESOURCES USING ARTIFICIAL INTELLIGENCE

By.

Jaswinder Singh Sekhon

DESIGN AND ANALYSIS OF HUMAN RESOURCES USING ARTIFICIAL INTELLIGENCE

By

Jaswinder Singh Sekhon

ABSTRACT

To analyze the work satisfaction enriches management with a variety of task, employee, environment, etc. knowledge which has made it easier to make decisions and to correct the course of organizational policy and actions. With the increase in global business activities, many companies expanding their business to overseas markets, Human Resource Management (HRM) is needed to make sure that they hire and retain well-performed employees. For a long time, companies/organizations have had big problems in getting accurate professionals to do the right work and training. The aim of this study is to design an automatic job satisfaction system using an optimized neural network approach. Initially, pre-processing is applied to the data to convert string data in terms of numeric data for fast computation purposes, and we change the name of "sales" by "Name of Department and "salary" by "low, medium, and high." The data analysis is performed based on three different factors, such as the number of employees in each department, the number of employees according to the salary range (low, medium, and high), and the number of employees according to the salary range and department. After this, we find out essential features (Satisfaction level and Last evaluation, Number of projects, Average monthly hours, Older employees with more than 10 years in the company), and then determine the correlation between these factors. Now, the Genetic Algorithm (GA) is applied as an optimization approach to enhance the quality of features. These optimal features are fed as input data to Artificial Neural Network (ANN), which is used for the prediction of employee's satisfaction level. At last, to show the effectiveness of the proposed work, a comparison between proposed GA with the ANN approach with the traditional GA with the K-means approach has been presented.

The considered parameters, such as Precision, Recall, and F-measure are measured to achieve the outcomes. Based on these factors, the satisfaction level predicted using three attributes passes as input data with multiple neurons in the hidden layer. Such parameters have been computed by taking different amount of elements such as 400, 600, 800 and 1000. To measure the performance of presented approach along with compare and analyse various in two phases; first computed the parameter value of GA and ANN separately and computed the value by making hybridization of GA with ANN in second phase, the comparison of

GA combining with K-means and GA ANN (Proposed Hybrid Approach). The average precision value by applying GA with K-means and GA- ANN for 400, 600, 800 and 1000 elements have been 95.41 and 96.74 correspondingly. The average recall value by applying GA with K-means and GA- ANN for 400, 600, 800 and 1000 elements have been 95.03 and 96.25. The average value of F-measure by applying GA with ANN corresponds to 400, 600, 800 and 1000 elements have been 96.58 and by applying GA with K-means has 95.395. The results show that the GA with the ANN prediction system has a better prediction effect with improved performance. To show the effectiveness of the proposed work, comparison with the SVM approach has also been presented. The improvement in precision, recall, and F-measure in the proposed work has been analyzed as 4.07 %, 2.05%, and 2.97 %, respectively, in contrast to the GA with the K-means approach.

TABLE OF CONTENTS

CERTIFICATE i

CERTIFICATE REGARDING ORIGINALITY OF WORK………………........................ii

ABSTARCT iii

ACKNOWLEDGEMENT... v

TABLE OF CONTENTS vi

LIST OF FIGURES.. ix

LIST OF TABLES..xiii

ABBREVIATIONS.. x

CHAPTER 1: INTRODUCTION .... **Error! Bookmark not defined.**

    1.1 EMPLOYEE SATISFACTION .... **Error! Bookmark not defined.**

    1.2 FACTOR AFFECTING JOB SATISFACTION .... **Error! Bookmark not defined.**

    1.3 HUMAN RESOURCE MANAGEMENT .... **Error! Bookmark not defined.**

        1.3.1 HUMAN RESOURCE MANAGEMENT DEFINITION..............................4

    1.4 FUNCTIONALITY OF HUMAN RESOURCE MANAGEMENT (HRM)**Error! Bookmark no**

    1.5 HISTORY IN MANAGEMENT OF HUMAN CAPITAL**Error! Bookmark not defined.**

    1.6 DIFFERENCE BETWEEN HUMAN RESOURCE MANAGEMENT AND PERSONAL MANAGEMENT………………….....…………………………....………..6

    1.7 ARTIFICIAL INTELLIGENCE...……………………………………….……………7

        1.7.1 GOAL OF ARTIFICIAL INTELLIGENCE 7

        1.7.2 FIELDS THAT FORM ARTIFICIAL INTELLIGENCE 7

1.7.3 WHAT IS INTELLIGENCE? 8

1.7.4 DIFFERENCE BETWEEN HUMAN AND ARTIFICIAL INTELLIGENCE 9

1.7.5 APPLICATIONS OF AI..10

1.7.6 FUNCTIONS OF ARTIFICIAL INTELLIGENCE IN HUMAN RESOURCES...12

1.7.7 WAYS AI MAY HELP HUMAN RESOURCES.......................................12

1.7.8 CHALLENGES OF AI IN HR DEPARMENT...13

1.8 GENETIC ALGORITHM (GA)..13

1.9 K-MEANS CLUSTERING 18

1.10 ARTIFICIAL NEURAL NETWORK (ANN).........**Error! Bookmark not defined.**

1.10.1 COMPONENTS OF ANN ....**Error! Bookmark not defined.**

1.10.2 TRAINING ANN ....**Error! Bookmark not defined.**

CHAPTER 2: LITERATURE REVIEW 24

2.1 GREEN HUMAN RESOURCE MANAGEMENT 27

CHAPTER 3: RESEARCH GAP AND PROBLEM FORMULATION 34

3.1 OBJECTIVES...35

CHAPTER 4: PROPOSED WORK 36

4.1 PROPOSED WORK FOR DEVELOPING HUMAN CAPITAL ANALYSIS.............36

4.1.1 ALGORITHM FOR PROPOSED WORK 38

4.1.2 ALGORITHM:OPTIMIZED FEATURE USING GA 39

4.2 EXPERIMENTAL SETUP 40

4.3 PROPOSED WORK FOR FORECASTING IN HUMAN RESOURCE PLANNING..45

4.3.1 ARTIFICIAL NEURAL NETWORK...46

4.3.1 a ALGORITHM: PREDICT SATISFACTION LEVEL USING ANN...........47

4.3.2 EXPERIMENTAL SETUP..48

CHAPTER 5: RESULT AND ANALYSIS 52

5.1 COMPARATIVE ANALYSIS.. 52

5.1.1 Computed parameters for 400Elements..53

5.1.1.1 Precision for 400 Elements 53

5.1.1.2 Recall for 400 Elements 54

5.1.1.3 F-measure for 400 Elements 55

5.1.2 Computed Parameters for 600 Elements 56

5.1.2.1 Precision for 600 elements... 56

5.1.2.2 Recall for 600 Elements... 58

5.1.2.3 F-measure for 600 Elements 59

5.1.3 Computed Parameters for 800 elements 60

5.1.3.1 Precision for 800 elements... 60

5.1.3.2 Recall for 800 Elements... 61

5.1.3.3 F-measure for 800 Elements 62

5.1.4 Computed Parameters for 1000 elements 63

5.1.4.1 Precision for 1000 Elements 64

5.1.4.2 Recall for 1000 Elements... 65

5.1.4.3 F-measure for 1000 Elements 66

5.2 TO COMPARE THE DEVELOPED SYSTEM WITH STATE OF ART TECHNIQUE COMPARISON OF GA WITH K-MEANS AND GA WITH ANN...................................67

5.2.1 Computed Parameters for 400 elements 67

5.2.1.1 Precision for 400 Elements 67

5.2.1.2 Recall for 400 Elements 69

5.2.1.3 F-measure for 400 Elements 70

5.2.2 Computed Parameter for 600 elements 71

5.2.2.1 Precision for 600 Elements 72

5.2.2.2 Recall for 600 Elements 73

5.2.2.3 F-measure for 600 Elements 74

5.2.3 Computed parameters for 800 elements 75

5.2.3.1 Precision for 800 Elements 75

5.2.3.2 Recall for 800 Elements 77

5.2.3.3 F-measure for 800 Elements 78

5.2.4 Computed Parameters for 1000 Elements. 79

5.2.4.1 Precision for 1000 Elements 79

5.2.4.2 Recall for 1000 Elements 80

5.2.4.3 F-measure for 1000 Elements 81

CHAPTER 6: CONCLUSION AND FUTURE SCOPE 83

    6.1 FUTURE SCOPE………………………………………………………………..84

REFERENCES 85

LIST OF FIGURES

Figure 1.1 Factor affecting Job satisfaction .... **Error! Bookmark not defined.**

Figure 1.2 Human Resource Management .... **Error! Bookmark not defined.**

Figure 1.3 Component of AI 7

Figure 1.4 Component of Intelligence 8

Figure 1.5 Instance of population, chromosome, gene, and allele. **Error! Bookmark not defined.**

Figure 1.6 GA Cycle .... **Error! Bookmark not defined.**

Figure 1.7 Example of the fitness function 16

Figure 1.8 One point crossover 17

Figure 1.9 Multipoint crossover 17

Figure 1.10 Uniform crossover 17

Figure 1.11 Euclidean Distance 18

Figure 1.12 Fitted data into K-means object 19

Figure 1.13 Clusters of data 19

Figure 1.14 Mathematical structure of ANN 21

Figure 1.15 Artificial Neural Network 21

Figure 1.16 Supervised Learning .... **Error! Bookmark not defined.**

Figure 1.17 Unsupervised Learning .... **Error! Bookmark not defined.**

Figure 4.1 Python dev environment 40

Figure 4.2 Spyder code unit 41

Figure 4.3 Category wise bifurcation 42

Figure 4.4 Updated Category value by GA 43

Figure 4.5 Scale Value 43

Figure 4.6 Classified Labels of Satisfaction 44

Figure 4.7 Selected Attributes Retrieved after GA 44

Figure 4.8 Training process of neural network 47

Figure 4.9 Total number of employees in each department 49

Figure 4.10 Total number of employees as per the range of salary i.e. low, medium and high ... 49

Figure 4.11 Total number of employees on the basis of defined range of salary and department 50

Figure 4.12 Monthly hours in average and total number of projects 50

Figure 4.13 Older employees including more than 10 years in company 51

Figure 4.14 Evaluation of Correlation 51

Figure 5.1 Precision for 400 Elements 53

Figure 5.2 Recall for 400 elements 54

Figure 5.3 F-measure for 400 Elements 56

Figure 5.4 Precision for 600 elements 57

Figure 5.5 Recall for 600 elements 58

Figure 5.6 F-measure for 600 Elements 59

Figure 5.7 Precision for 800 elements 61

Figure 5.8 Recall for 800 elements 62

Figure 5.9 F-measure for 800 Elements 63

Figure 5.10 Precision for 1000 Elements 64

Figure 5.11 Recall for 1000 Elements 65

Figure 5.12 F-measure for 1000 Elements 66

Figure 5.13 Precision for 400 Elements 68

Figure 5.14 Recall for 400 Elements 69

Figure 5.15 F-measure for 400 Elements 71

Figure 5.16 Precision for 600 Elements 72

Figure 5.17 Recall for 600 Elements 73

Figure 5.18 F-measure for 600 Elements 74

Figure 5.19 Precision for 800 Elements 76

Figure 5.20 Recall for 800 Elements 77

Figure 5.21 F-measure for 800 Elements 78

Figure 5.22 Precision for 1000 Elements 80

Figure 5.23 Recall for 1000 Elements 81

Figure 5.24 F-measure for 1000 Elements 82

LIST OF TABLES

Table 1.1 Difference between Human and Artificial Intelligence 9

Table 2.1 Discussion of Existing Work 28

Table 4.1 Dataset 37

Table 5.1 Precision for 400 Elements 53

Table 5.2 Recall for 400 elements 54

Table 5.3 F-measure for 400 Elements 55

Table 5.4 Precision for 600 elements 57

Table 5.5 Recall for 600 elements 58

Table 5.6 F-measure for 600 Elements 59

Table 5.7 Precision for 800 elements 60

Table 5.8 Recall for 800 elements 61

Table 5.9 F-measure for 800 Elements 62

Table 5.10 Precision for 1000 elements 64

Table 5.11 Recall for 1000 Elements 65

Table 5.12 F-measure for 1000 Elements 66

Table 5.13 Precision for 400 Elements 67

Table 5.14 Recall for 400 Elements 69

Table 5.15 F-measure for 400 Elements 70

Table 5.16 Precision for 600 Elements 72

Table 5.17 Recall for 600 Elements 73

Table 5.18 F-measure for 600 Elements 74

Table 5.19 Precision for 800 Elements 75

Table 5.20 Recall for 800 Elements 77

Table 5.21 F-measure for 800 Elements 78

Table 5.22 Precision for 1000 Elements 79

Table 5.23 Recall for 1000 Elements 80

Table 5.24 F-measure for 1000 Elements 81

ABBREVIATIONS

GUI-Graphical User Interface

RAM-Random Access Memory

HRM – Human Resource Management

AI – Artificial Intelligence

GA – Genetic Algorithm

ANN – Artificial Neural Network

SVM- Support Vector Machine

DT – Decision Trees

RF- Random Forest

ML- Machine Learning

LR- Logistic Regression

KNN- K NearestNeighbors

GBM- Gradient Boosting Machine

AUC-Area Under ROC Curve

MSE-Mean Squared Error

OCBE-Organizational Citizenship Behaviour

LDA- Linear Discriminant Analysis

NB- Naïve Bayes

PPV- Positive Predictive Value

SHRM- Strategic Human Resource Management

FS- Featured Set

CO- Crossover Operators

MU- Mutation Operators

OFS- Optimized Feature Set

CHAPTER 1: INTRODUCTION

1.1 EMPLOYEE SATISFACTION

Workers happiness or work contentment depends how happy, pleased workers are in there jobs. Satisfaction at the workplace is typically measured using a survey. Factors that impact workplace retention discussed in such surveys may involve remuneration, load, administration, prospects, accessibility, collaboration, infrastructure (Siregar et al. 2020).

These things are essential in organizations that want to maintain their employees happy. Satisfaction doesn't compensate for good efficiency or dedication. HR concepts and approaches based on how workplace retention can be increased also provide outcomes that demoralize top performers.

Employee happiness and employee participation on the surface are related words and often use both definitions interchangeably. For an organization to make rational choices and build a climate of involvement, the value of understanding the difference between happiness and dedication is important. Satisfaction of workers encompasses key employee interests and needs. It's a decent point of departure, but typically doesn't matter. There are three important dimensions of job satisfaction (Silic et al. 2020).

- Work satisfaction cannot be seen; it can be assumed only. This is critical when it comes to ones attitude to work.
- Work satisfaction also determines how well the results fulfill the needs of people and how well expectations are met. If employees working in the company believe like they are working much more than others in the organization but they are not getting the promotion or better compensation, they will become frustrated with the job, the manager, and co-workers. If employee thinks that they are being paid equal wages and being given satisfactory working atmosphere, they will be happy. .

- Employment satisfaction is one of the desirable outcomes for workers. This is conceptually equal to w satisfaction and job dissatisfaction.

These two words are often confused to be the same, however, they actually have a difference in meaning. Employment satisfaction is closely linked to attitudes. Attitudes depend on attitudes toward hierarchical entities and objects. Job satisfaction applies to job satisfaction. Attitudes refer to reaction but satisfaction refers to success factors. Attitudes are long-lasting, but satisfaction varies with the situation. It is expected to decline much more rapidly than it began. Managers need to note that job satisfaction is essential to a workers' long-term loyalty.

1.2 FACTOR AFFECTING JOB SATISFACTION

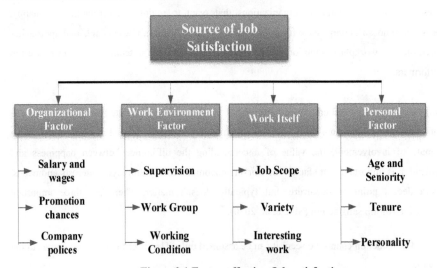

Figure 0.1 Factor affecting Job satisfaction

1.3 HUMAN RESOURCE MANAGEMENT

HRM is the way to hire and pay staff, establish strategies and develop methods of employee retention .(Noe et al. 2007) the past many years, HRM has endured several changes and has played an even greater role in organizations today. In p history, HRM included compensation handling, supplying staff with holidays gifts, arranging customer activiti and ensuring that documentation was properly done. organizations today require strategic position that is essential to the company's success in hiring.

Hunan Resource Management is a combination of three different meanings depicting works. Person refers the professional workers of an organisation, Assets relate to restricted or insufficient resources, Leadership refers to how to manage and allow effective use of that finite resource such that the company fulfils the intended purpose or target.

Figure 0.2 Human Resource Management

The management of human resources is thus meant for the best use of the professional staff available and the successful use of experienced personnel within the company (Rao et al. 2009). In the current case, the main explanation is that the building sector experienced a severe lack of qualified workers. In the coming decade, it is projected to triple from 30 percent today. The total output of the sector would have a negative effect, say industry experts.

1.3.1 Human Resource Management Definition

Many authors have described HRM in numerous forms , but the central definition of HRM is how people or workers are handled in the enterprise. (Obedgiu, V. (2017).

HRM is narrated by **Edwin Flippo** as' composing, arranging, managing of human resources to achieve goals.' "Human resources-personal management has been defined by the National Institute of Personal Management (NIPM) of India as "the part of management that concerns employees at work and their temperament within an enterprise. Its goal is to put together and grow the men and women who make up the business a successful enterprise , considering wellbeing of groups and individuals.

Decenzo and Robbins state that HRM is concerned with the human aspect of a process. You have to cultivate talents of and company, promote and sustain their contribution to the enterprise in order to attain institution's goals. Despite its form, democracy, education, and social action must be maintained.

1.4 FUNCTIONALITY OF HUMAN RESOURCE MANAGEMENT (HRM)

Management of resources involves functions such as planning, organizing, directing and controlling (Longoni et al. 2018)

- It Comprises acquisition, development, employee routine maintenance.
- It Supports the achievement of personal, institutional and community objectives.
- It includes studies on management research , philosophy, interaction and economy.
- Team spirit and team effort are involved in this.

1.5 HISTORY IN MANAGEMENT OF HUMAN CAPITAL

Management of human resources has grown from the Personnel Administration system. To know the nature of personnel administration one needs to pay attention the past and reaction of centuries of human behavior studies by leading psychologists. Elton Mayo an Australian researcher, who in 1924 made several studies on human actions in multiple circumstances. He strongly believed in the harmony between work and life to enhance the potency of employees and concentrated on human relationships that impacted the productivity of employees and was ultimately known as the father of human resource management. (Cooke et al. 2020), (Onyusheva et al. 2017), (Marler, J. H. 2012)

In the course of history, management of human resources has evolved many times in name. The name changed due to the historical changes in communal and economy activities.

- **Industrial Welfare**

The first way to handle human capital was industrial well-being (HRM). The Act of 1833 specified that manufacturers should be male inspectors. In 1878 the law governing working hours for minors and females was introduced at 60 hours a week .Organized labour began to grow through this period. The 1st trade-union congress was conducted in 1868. That was the beginning of joint negotiations. The amount of industrial welfare employees had increased so a conference was held in 1913, arranged by Sebum Rowntree.

- **Recruitment and Preference**

It commenced when Mary Wood was ordered to begin involving girls in the First World War. Personnel development increased in the First World War due to public programs to foster people's best usage. Having a welfare worker in explosive factories became compulsory in 1916, and was encouraged in factories for munitions. In this sector, the military has worked extensively. The army focused on assessing capabilities and intelligence in addition to other research on human behavior at job. In 1921, the National Institute of Psychologists developed and released research of studies on measures of quality, communication approaches and methods of preparation.

- **Industrial Relation**

Consultation was spread with management and workers in the war. This meant, the management offices were responsible for planning and handling it. Health and safety was a concern and a need for experts. The need for practitioners to work on labor issues was known to be such that, although talks were being held with trade unions/shop stewards, the staff manager was the spokeswoman of the company. Industrial relations became very significant in the 1970s. The warm climate during this period also demonstrated the importance of a skilled role in the management of labor relations. The Recruiting Officer was encouraged to explore pay rates and other community concerns.

- **Flexibility and Diversity**

A substantial change occurred in the 1990s when employers sought to enhance the flexibility of employees' of employment as a result of the rise in part-time positions and the advent of distance work. Workforce an habits became more complex where conventional recruiting methods got futile. Rise of Internet usage in the 2000 demanded a transition to the world of 24/7. It has provided new opportunities in e-commerce, wh traditional places such as shops have lost their jobs. This also suggested an improvement in the capacity c workplace to function from home. Organizations should take a critical view of the issues arising from developments. The role of the HRM manager can change with changes occurring.

Some of the systems where HRM is sponsored by IT are: e-recruitment systems, short listing of appli ,online assessment strategies, payroll systems and pre-recruiting assessments. IT helps managers to pe repetitive activities that will allow them to tackle challenging problems with flexibility. IT always mean more knowledge is available for decision-making.

1.6 DIFFERENCE BETWEEN HUMAN RESOURCE MANAGEMENT AND PERSO MANAGEMENT

Personnel management acts as the kernel of HRM. It can be stated that HRM is built from the managing employees. The core concept of the management of staff is to get work done from an employee for the salary given. Employees were not granted that much importance in the decision-making system during the Personne Management period and were not permitted to communicate with higher management. Personnel managemer restricted to factories and the personal manager's primary concern was to see if everything met with labor law not, not much importance was put on employee morale. Employees were only viewed as resources, the organization's responsibility, in addition to being seen as expense & expenditure to the business rather than capital and future asset. The most widely used staff officers are punitive rather than versatile and cooperative staff. Employee nurturing was not a concern for staff managers and the opinion of workers was overlooked, meaning employee managers rather than recognizing the situation they used to be punitive if the employee m any mistake. (Tutar et al. 2020).

Viewpoint of HRM is that, workers are company's most important resources and they regard their employees value of assets for their organization. In comparison to personal management, empowering workers is a fundamental aspect of HRM. The core notion of managing human resources is seeing what should be provide an employee to extract the desired job. Employee engagement in decision-making is often welcomed by HR managers and their opinions are most respected. Employee versatility in job and health is an important aspect HR executives and they show more importance about employee problems. New regulations and enhancemen approaches are well supported and easy to enforce by the Hr Manager. The key difference between staff management and human human resources management was the incorporation and strengthening of informatic technology into HR process and functions for better productivity and time savings. Artificial intelligence and Robots take over many HR roles, ranging from recruiting of staff, research, interviewing and many more.

1.7 ARTIFICIAL INTELLIGENCE

Expert systems is the automated mirroring of natural intelligence processes (Wirtz et al. 2019). The capacity of a computer system or a computer-driven machine to perform smart tasks. It was found that expert systems can now map out highly compound activities, such as playing chess, with great skill following the first computer breakthrough in the 1940s. (Kouziokas, G. N. (2017). Nonetheless, given ongoing improvements in machine speed and memory power, no applications are yet accessible that can equal human autonomy across larger realms or activities involving a great deal of everyday information.

1.7.1 Goal of Artificial Intelligence

- To Create Expert Systems — The programs that show smart behavior, understand, illustrate, clarify and inform the consumers.

- To Implement Natural Intelligence in Machines — Build systems which understand and act like Natural beings.

1.7.2 Fields that form Artificial Intelligence

Artificial intelligence is focused on fields such as computational science genetics, psychiatry etc. AI's main goal is the creation of computer functions, like reasoning, understanding and problem solving correlated with human intelligence. (Ayoub et al. 2016).

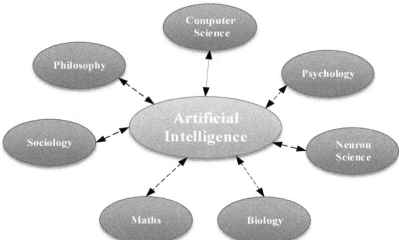

Figure 0.3 Component of AI

1.7.3 What is Intelligence

Knowledge can be described as the easiest human action although only the most complex insect activity is rare taken as an indicator of intellect. Consider the digger wasp behavior, Sphex ichneumons. Once the female wasp returns with food to her burrow, she first positions it on the threshold, searches for intruders inside her burrow, and then then, when the shore is open, takes her food inside.

The true essence of the instinctual actions of the wasp is exposed as the food is pushed a few inches away from the entrance to its burrow when it is inside: as it returns, it can replicate the same process as much when the food is transferred. Intelligence — notably missing in Sphex's case — must have the opportunity to respond to new situations.

. In general, psychologists do not describe human intellect by a given attribute, but by a mixture of several different skills. AI focused primarily on the following knowledge components listening, reasoning, problem-solving, understanding, and language.

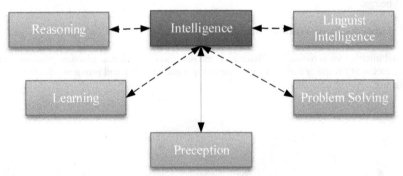

Figure 0.4 Component of Intelligence

   i. **Learning**

When applied to artificial intelligence, there are many various ways of learning open. The easiest of these is to know by hit and error. For eg, a computer program to solve chess problems might attempt random moves before the match. The device should therefore archive each answer with the destination in such a way that it remember the answer the upcoming time the machine finds the same destination. The simple recalling of objects is called rotational learning The problem is more difficult to apply what is called generalization. Generalization means adapting previous experience to current comparable circumstances. For example, a system that knows the past tense of standard English verbs, won't be able to generate the past tense of a term such as jumping until it was already provided with jumping, while a system that will generalize will learn the "add ed" rule and thereby shap the past tense of jumping based on familiarity with related verbs.

   ii. **Reasoning**

The aim is to draw the necessary conclusions to the case. Assumptions are either inductive or deductive. One example is, "Fred has to be either in the museum or the cafe. He's not in the café; thus, he's in the museum," an from the above, "previous injuries of this nature were triggered by failure. The most important distinction in bo types of logic is that the validity of the assumption assures the reality of the inference in the deductive situation, while in the inductive situation the validity of the hypothesis confirms the claim by providing full certainty.Inductive inference is popular in research, where data are gathered, and preliminary models are built to explain and forecast potential behavior — until anomalous data presence causes the model to be updated.

iii. Problem Solving

Solving problems in AI, can be summarized as a systemic quest over a set of potential acts to achieve any predefined objective or solution. Techniques for problem solving split between specific use and general one . A specially modified approach is adapted to a specific issue and also takes benefit of very specific circumstances in which the issue is incorporated.

iv. Perception

In vision, the environment is mediated by various sensory components, whether actual or virtual, and the image is separated into separate objects in unique complex cognition. Research is complicated by the fact that an object can appear different from the viewpoint from which it is viewed, the location and intensity of the lighting in the scene, and the contrast between the entity and the external environment

v. Language

A lingo is a collection of signals which have traditional significance. Language in that context shouldn't be limited to the uttered word. For example, travel signs form a language, which is a matter of tradition, which in some countries means risk ahead.

1.7.4   Difference Between Human and Artificial Intelligence. (Yawalkar, M. V. V. (2019), Rani, S
Table 0.1 Difference between Human and Artificial Intelligence

S. No.	Features	Artificial Intelligence	Human Intelligence
1.	Emergence	AI is an improvement in human observations.	Human intelligence is created with the ability to consider, reason and analyze, etc..
2.	Speed of Calculation	Compared to humans, more data can be handled by machines more easily. If a mathematical problem can be solved by the human intelligence within 5 minutes, AI can overcome 10 problems in one minute.	Humans cannot beat the speed of machine.
3.	Decision Making	AI is can make decisions without influence.	Individual decisions can be influenced by specific components which are not dependent on statistics alone.

4.	Energy Consumption	On an average AI consume about 2 watts of energy for doing a piece of work.	For the same piece of work human brain can consumed about 25 watt of energy.
5.	Modification or adaptation of new Environment	AI take much more time to adapt new environment or to adjust.	Human perspectives can be adaptable in response to changes in the climate. This makes individuals able to recite and master various abilities.

1.7.5 APPLICATIONS OF AI

In a large range of industries, artificial intelligence has found its way. Here are some of the examples .(SUBASHINI, G. 2020)

- **AI in healthcare.**

The objective is to boost medical contentment and cut prices. Enterprises detect patterns to render diagnostics safer and quicker than humans. IBM Watson understands the natural language and can reply to queries that are put. The system creates a hypothesis from the available healthcare data and then represents the scenario with a scoring scheme. Many AI softwares use advanced digital health bots to help patients and health care clients fin diagnostic records, arrange appointments and complete other work processes. In order to know, battle and understand epidemics such as COVID-19, an array of AI systems are also being used.

- **AI in business.**

In order to discover information about how to provide direct support to clients, chatbots have been integrated in websites. Academics and IT analysts have also been a talking point in the automation of work positions.

- **AI in Education**

AI will simplify evaluation, providing ample time to instructors. It will analyze and adjust students to their requirements, allowing them to function at their own speed. Teachers will provide students with extra support that they can focus more.

- **AI in finance**

AI is changing the banking industry through goods such as Mint or TurboTax. Applications like these collect a offer financial advice on personal data. The method of purchasing a home has been extended to other services, such as IBM Watson. Artificial intelligence systems today carry out most of the Wall Street business.

- **AI in law**

There are several records and testimony to access in rule. AI helps simplify the labor-intensive processes of the legal industry which improves client support. Law enterprises are using ML techniques to explain data and forecast results, computer vision techniques to identify documents and pull out knowledge from them.

- **AI in manufacturing**

Manufacturing has been at the top of the list of industrial and scientific use of robots. Take for example this cobot that could handle more parts of a single or multiple tasks as in modern workplaces.

- **AI in banking**

Banks are effective because of the automated chatbots that conduct transactions that require no human interaction. Digital assistants help deduct enforcement bills of banking regulations. Banks use artificial intelligence to make loan decisions and to determine upon creditworthiness of its customers.

- **AI in transportation**

In addition to AI's core function in autonomous vehicles, AI is also used in moving , such as forecasting traffic, planning delayed flights and increasing the productivity of ocean shipping.

- **AI in security**

Automation and machine learning have become big buzzwords in the field of network security. These are not only theories but also practical technology. Artificial intelligence and machine learning are bringing real value to the security field by detecting the attacks, malware and other risks.The SIEM software uses machine learning methods to identify suspicious activities. By collecting information from different sources, A.I. will detect links to events and attack campaigns. Thus, AI security technology both significantly lowers the chance of frauds and authenticates deals faster. The maturing technology is critical for organizations to combat cyber-attacks.

1.7.6 Functions of Artificial Intelligence in Human Resources

HR department now a day's are heading into digital revolution by using various methods to simplify work through big data analytics ,artificial intelligence and cloud computing. Most of the companies used arti intelligence or HR bots today. Artificial intelligence can play a major role in human resource management.

1. Companies should use digital technologies for recruitments, so that they can have more successful outcor chat bot system plays an important role in an organisation's recruiting process.

2. By using AI technology, the screening process is simplified because it eliminates human effort. Amy and are software tools used to arrange interviews and work sessions.

3. organizations use automation and artificial intelligence, therefore, employers can reduce the administ burden. AI technology provides problem solving and increases productivity of HR in an enterprise.

4. Researchers (Rajesh et al. 2018) explored how AI can successfully streamline employee assessment systen

5. AI is used to make sure there are no favoritism in the business. An company should hire workers based on credentials and skill.

6. AI would bring about greater efficiencies in the business. Various robotic operations have been undertak order to boost workplace efficiency. ,these tasks include collection of information, observation , categori sorting, entry of the data into HR and payroll systems etc.

7. The use of computers and emerging technologies would be improved. The use of machines and compute different industries ensures that statistics and feedback can be obtained fast and easily. Microsoft 365 prin allow workers to save time and reduce the expenses.

1.7.7 Ways AI may help Human Resource.

1. Decrease the pressure on company management personnel.

2. Identify the best applicants for the job.

3. AI helps forecast work retention rates.

4. It can transcend human weaknesses and function accordingly.

5. The workflow will be maintained in different departments.

6. Accurate results can be obtained by AI firms.

7. It will improve the participation of workers in the organization.

8. It will help decrease bias in judgment.

1.7.8 Challenges of AI in HR departments.

In the modern enterprise, there is substantial presence of AI in the human resources department. Most of the time it becomes hard for workers to embrace and to use AI tools and skills in emerging technology. AI would play a big role in the industry because it changes people's minds too much. It will be very necessary for HR department to recruit the right person who can handle AI systems. Another restriction for HR is to make day-to-day decision as HR would lose its authority and power as HR becomes incapable to take major decisions.

1.8 GENETIC ALGORITHM (GA)

GA is a tool for addressing, constrained and unregulated development issues on the basis of a ordinary selection mechanism that replicates biological development. The algorithm updates a sequence of results. The genetic algorithm picks individuals from the population at each step and uses the same as parents for next-generation children (Manoj et al. 2010). This optimization approach is driven by a random search and one of the most common optimization techniques for multi-objective optimization problems under evolution algorithms. Genetic algorithms have been found to be able to find solutions to a wide range of problems, for which algorithmic solutions are not acceptable. GA is a random search approach whose working performance is based on the natural selection strategy. This techniques combines the concept of Drawin's to get the structural knowledge transformation by using operators which is helpful into the evaluation of an effective search algorithm. In this optimization approach, an individual is abstracted as a chromosome that composed of genotype (coding), by which phenotype (solution) for a particular problem. Such individualis particularly implemented as a vector, list or set of gene. In this algorithm having enormous ways to simulate the behaviour, individuals can be selected randomly from the population among those, the one having best fitness values are chosen to perform the crossover. The numbers of children's are increased by making a combination of genes between parents. If there is two chromosomes are given then a position known as cut-off point is selected. After that exchange is performed in which the first chromosomes interchange the posterior subset to the cut-off point through second chromosomes which produces two new individuals (HANDA, D. (2014)).

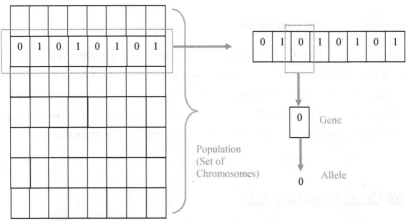

Figure 0.5 Instance of population, chromosome, gene, and allele

The terms used in the genetic algorithms are discussed below :

I. **Population:** Most commonly utilized term denotes the group of all probable coded solutions for specified problem and it is similar to the population of human. Additionally, to replace humans, have candidate solutions for representing the humans.

II. **Chromosomes:** It corresponds to one of the solutions towards the assigned problem.

III. **Gene:** It denotes the location of particular element in chromosome.

IV. **Allele:** It tends to the value of gene considered for particular chromosome.

V. **Fitness function**: This is defined as a function which calculates the fitness of the bits so that they can be further processed.

VI. **Genetic operators of GA**: Crossover, mutation, and selection.

VII. **Genotype**: Density in computational area. In this area numerical effects can be easily simulated by using a computer machine

VIII. **Phenotype**: It represents the true solution in such a way that it appears in the real world.

More importantly, GA is consumed to solve the optimization problems in few steps as illustrated in working cycle in figure 1.6.

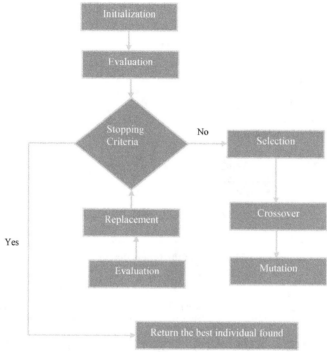

Figure 0.6 GA Cycle

https://www.gatevidyalay.com/genetic-algorithm-in-ai-operators-working/.

1. **Initialization of population**

   Population is characterized as "all probable coded solution to a problem." It is equivalent to the human population. We have candidate solutions, in addition to replace humans, that reflect humans.

2. **Fitness Function**

It is a function in GA to get optimized value of a solution, such that the other chromosomes can be arranged against anyone. Particularly it used for selection of best chromosomes which is utilized for the offspring reproduction; thus by almost all chromosomes, an evaluation criterion is provided. The obtained value by fitness function is consumed to choose the individuals which are used for further process of reproduction.

A fitness function may have the following two characteristics:.
- Computation must be quick.
- This process decides the best value to be allocated to a problem.

The example of determining the fitness value is shown below:

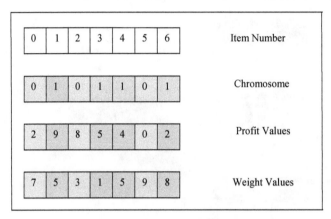

Figure 0.7 Example of the fitness function

3. Selection

It is the method of choosing two or more crossbreeding parents from the population. That is responsible to determine how execute selection, i.e. how to select individuals in the population who will generate offspring for the next generation and how many offspring each will make. The aim of the selection is to accentuate the individuals that the population hopes th jumps will be more efficient. From the initial population chromosomes are selected to be reproductive parents. The probl is how it selects chromosomes. The best thing to do is to create something new, in accordance with Darwin's theory of evolution. Specifically, this phase is performed to determine the area from where one can get a best solution in large amount. In which the key objective of GA is to shift genotype towards the enhanced fitness evaluation within the availab search space. The selection of fitness function is done in such a way by which more accurate solution is obtained accordi as per the requirements.

4. Reproduction

Select Reproduction individuals with high fitness values in the population, and a new population is derived from cross-breeding and mutation in such individuals in which individuals fit into their environment even better. In GA optimizer, th offspring reproduction is performed by utilizing crossover and mutation. Among them crossover is consumed for selectic of random point during the formation of parents in the process of offspring generation. Crossover may be available in single-point, two-point and uniform and the generated offspring is combined into the population.

   i. **Mutation**

The representation of mutation can be as a small arbitrary adaptation, considered the chromosome for a new solution to be obtained. It is used to protect the diversity of the human population, and is typically introduced with less chance. The genetic algorithm will decrease after random search, if the possibility is greater.

ii. Crossover

Reproduction and biological crossover are close to that of hybridization. More than one parent with more than one offsprings are observed. This argument is applicable to high-probability situations.
The cross-controllers are discussed next, as well as the example:
    a. One point crossover.

Therefore, the mode of crossover depends on the number of chromosomes per offspring.

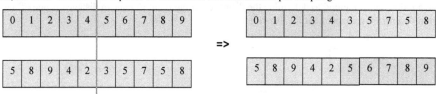

Figure 0.8 One point crossover

    a. Multipoint crossover

. In this process, upwards of one crossover point is used to estimate the offspring value.

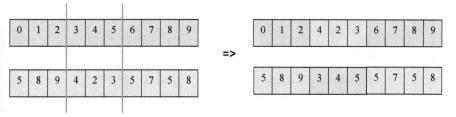

Figure 0.9 Multipoint crossover

    b. Uniform crossover

Chromosomes are not broken into segments and the genes are viewed individually.

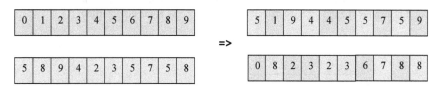

Figure 0.10 Uniform crossover

1.9 K-MEANS CLUSTERING

The division of data point into homogeneous classes or groups is done through a clustering strategy. Centroid of the group of data is located by clustering approach, to generate effective clustering evaluation of distance between each point from centroid of the cluster is performed. K-means clustering is one of the simplest unsupervised algorithms by which problem clustering has been resolved.(Kavya et al. 2016). This clustering approach is a method of vector quantization. K-means clustering partitions the data into clusters in the way of data points with similar features involved in the same cluster and data points with different features are stored in distinct clusters.
There are number of method to determine the distance among them Euclidean distance is one of the most commonly utilized measurement for distance.

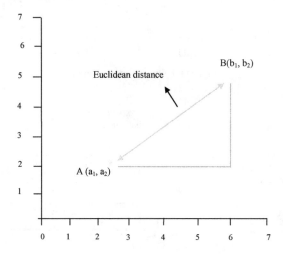

Figure 0.11 Euclidean Distance

As shown in figure 1.11, the computation of Euclidean distance among two points in 2-dimensional space is by using the square of the difference between x and y coordinates of the points.
Euclidean distance is an ideal metric for geometrical queries. Euclidean distance can be defined as the straight line distance between two points. Euclidean distance is commonly used for clustering analysis, including clustering text. It is also the regular distance calculation applied to the K-means algorithm.

$$Euclidean\ distance = \sqrt{(a_1 - b_1)^2 + (a_2 - b_2)^2}$$

K-means clustering always tries to reduce the distance inside a same cluster along with increases the distance among different cluster (Gupta et al. 2020)

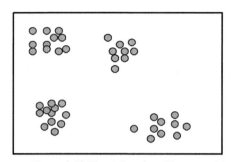

Figure 0.12 Fitted data into K-means object

As depicted in figure 1.12 the collection of datasets is available in large amount the needs to be cluster among different group for further processing of data to utilize task.

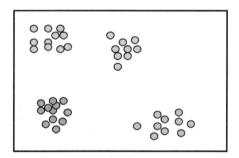

Figure 0.13 Clusters of data

As given in figure 1.13 the huge amount of datasets are clustered among four groups which represented by different colors according to their behaviours. As K-means clustering is not able to define the number of clusters so it requires determining the value of 'K' during creation of K-means object which is very challenging task. K-means is an iterative process that builds on expectation-maximization approach. The algorithm of clustering K-means is incremental for finishing the result. The inputs to the algorithm are the amount of clusters and the data collection. The data is a set of attributes for each data point. After determining the number of clusters (K) its working is done by executing the below given steps;

    i.   The algorithm initializes with estimations for the K-centroids which can be generated randomly or selected randomly from the datasets objects, here centroids are also sounds as center of cluster.

    ii.   Calculation of distance for all data points to the center of cluster.

iii. One of the clusters is defined by each cluster and each data point is assigned to its nearest centr on the basis of squared Euclidean distance. Moreover, if is corresponding to the collect of centroids in set (Y), then each data point X is assigned to a cluster on the basis of

$$\underset{c_i \in Y}{\arg\min} \; dist(c_i, x)^2$$

In which dist (·) is corresponding to the standard Euclidean distance. Lets us assumes that the of data point assignments for each cluster at position centroid is .

iv. Calculation of new cntroids for each cluster which is performed by taking the mean of t number of data points that are allocated to that particular centroid's cluster.

$$C_i = \frac{1}{|S_i|} \sum_{X_i \in S_i} X_i$$

v. Repeat the steps in the middle of both steps 2, 3 and 4 until a mending condition come across (means, none of the data points convert clusters, the sum of the distances is minimized, nearly maximum number of iterations is arrived).

1.10 ARTIFICIAL NEURAL NETWORK (ANN)

ANN is biologically motivated computing system. ANN systems rely on the interconnected nodes or units that also known as artificial neurons that are roughly equivalent to the neuron of the biological nervous system. The signals are processed through the neurons connections that are equivalent to the synapses found in brain. By default a neural network consists of input layer, invisible layer and output layer with connections (Pagariya et 2013).The definition of ANN can be provided as systems to computing systems by which simulate the structure of brain system. To perform particular task data is elaborate from input parameters.

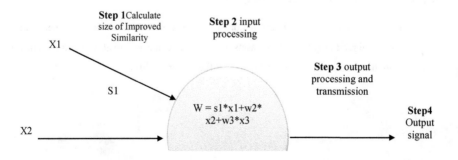

Figure 0.14 Mathematical structure of ANN

As given in figure 1.14, the term 'S1', 'S2', and 'S3' provide the strength of the input signal. In step 1, computes size of similarity by using the input 'X1', 'X2' and, 'X3' and strength of input signal. In step 2 and step 3 performs processing of input and produces corresponding output. One of the specialties of neural networks is that the hidden unit's factors.

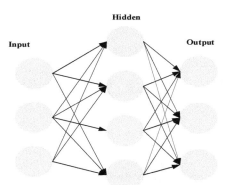

Figure 0.15 Artificial Neural Network

ANN has been employed to offer solution to tackle social network, medical diagnosis, speech recognition, computer vision, playing games and machine translation problems. The neurons are connected while employing various patterns such that output from some neurons is used as the input other neurons and results in a network of weighed graphs.

1.10.1 Components of ANN (Dharwal et al. 2016)

- **Neurons**

These are the functional entities that receive the input, combine them when get activated to attain a threshold value and process the output on the basis of output function. The inputs here used to be images or the text documents that are processed to accomplish some image processing or classification tasks. The activation function here holds a very important position as they govern the smooth transition and relationship between input and output values.

- **Connections or links**

The network is represented as a interconnected network of neurons. Input of one neuron layer is connected to another neuron. These connections are assigned weights that corresponds to their inherit importance. There may be multiple input and output connections for a single neuron.

- **Propagation Function**

The function is used to read input from the neuron and process it and transmit the computed results to the next neuron. Sometime bias can be observed during the propagation of information and results.

- **Transfer function**

It used to transfer the message after processing element been processed and produce the range of message between [1, 0] or, [1, 1] as the output message. Without using transfer the network output may be very large as well as complexity is increased for overall network.

1.10.2 Training ANN

The training needs of ANN are focused on certain processes of learning. The network is compelled to respond particular inputs using training techniques It becomes important when knowledge is limitless or imperfect.

- **Supervised learning**

In this method, we imagine that the necessary system feedback is obtained at each time the input is used (Lloyd al. 2013). The outcome of an established example it attempts to predict. These systems equate their forecasts with known outcomes and learn from errors.. The design is shown in Figure1.16.

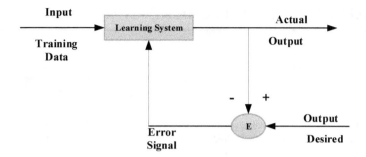

Figure 0.16 Supervised Learning

Weight is thus modified to minimize the difference between desired input and specified output.

- **Unregulated learning**

The requested response is unknown in the learning process, and thus the failure signal cannot be used to enhance the network behavior. Since the answer is not right or reliable, we can learn on the evidence of our monitoring answers to our nominal or ignorant inputs.

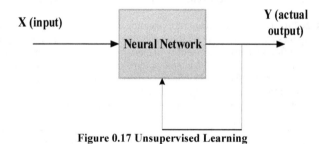

Figure 0.17 Unsupervised Learning

Figure 1.17, shows that unsupervised learning process does not use any feedback algorithm.

CHAPTER 2: LITERATURE REVIEW

This lesson presents a comprehensive literature survey of the algorithms proposed in the past regarding the proposed work, their outcome, drawbacks, etc. It highlights the research work done by various eminent researchers in the related and allied fields. It also explores some prevailing issues that need to be resolved..

(Chaudhary.R (2020) demonstrated an appreciation of the role of GHRM in supporting employee environmental efficiency. The study highlights the part of HRM in attaining environmental longevity and stre the urgency to integrate feasibility into HR processes in order to garner sustainable development goals. In thi study, the writer proves that GHRM is one of the techniques to foster and facilitate certain attitudes and behaviours; thus, enterprises should implement successful "green" policies in the HRM context to achieve the green performance objectives.

(Ho et al. 2020) looks into the effects of HRM on employee well being, and subsequent firm results. Researc vary on the effect of HRM systems on employee well-being and the impact of such systems on firms efficien Researchers assert that employers and workers both benefit from HRM systems (i.e., the mutual gains perspective). On the other side of the continuum, researchers assert that employers, but not workers, have advantage from HRM systems.

(Yanli et al. 2020) illustrated an empirical study by questionnaire surveying 779 companies across China on conciliating role of human capital in association with the management structure of human resources and sustainable competitive advantage of companies. Results show that, first, for businesses to follow a varie strategies, the HRM system and human capital must be separated, and secondly, different forms of human resources have a different energy effectiveness in various aggressive strategies.

(Sabuhari et al. 2020) aims at researching and evaluating the impact on employee efficiency of versatility in area of human resources and skills, adapting the organization's culture and satisfying employees. The study a looks at the indirect influence between versatility in human resources and employee performance through a variable mediation of adaptation of organizational culture and the effect of competence on the performance o employees by means of job satisfaction. The findings showed that work satisfaction was able to influence employee output part of the impact of competence. Some workers may increase their efficiency if they are ha with their jobs. Results showed that ability is more important than HR versatility in terms of employee efficie

(Davidescu et al. 2020) examined the links between employees' growth, workplace flexibility, and workplac flexibility as important properties for Romanian employees' sustainable HRM, job satisfaction, and job perfo Furthermore, the purpose of the study is to investigate the effect on employee growth and employee flexibilit essential aspects of sustainable HRM in improving the overall level of employee satisfaction, of various flexibilities, contractual, work time and workplace flexibility. In addition, the effect on the overall job satisfa of individual as well as employee flexibility was quantified using binary logistical regression models.

(Boon et al. 2019) extended the spectrum of HCHR's fitness with other elements of the human resources management framework to incorporate previous conceptualizations of fitness within the Strategic Human Resources (HR) literature. The author hypothesizes a number of relationships that can arise when a firm uses framework of HIPRE practices and has a charismatic leader, efficiency is highest and turnover lowest.

(Saeed et al. 2019) built and validated a model that positively link green HRM practices with staff pro-ambient actions and improves the coordination between green HRM practices. The findings were that green human resource management strategies contribute to workers' pro-environmental actions and that pro-environmental mental capital mediates this connection. Environmental consciousness has a moderating impact on pro-environmental actions.

(Chams et al. 2019) explored SHRM's central position in creating and promoting the achievement of SDGs in a healthy working climate. This analysis identifies the history and findings of SHRM and highlights, on the basis of a collection of the conceptual and methodological papers, the barriers to sustainable adoption not only at company level, but also globally.

(Otoo 2019) explores the role of moderator in the interaction between HRM and organisation's performance of employee competences. The combination of key factors in current literature established an integrated research model. Data have been obtained from 600 workers of the selected hotels via a questionnaire. The model validity and hypotheses were checked by structural modeling equation. Confirmatory factor analysis evaluates the strength and accuracy of the dimensions. The findings show that some HRM behaviors affect organizational efficiency by affecting employee abilities.

(Jawaad et al. 2019) integrated Organizational justice, workers perceived organizational support, work satisfaction and affective organizational engagement and how they respond to information sharing behaviors. In addition, the perceptions of organizational justice can have a positive effect on perceived organizational support, which can, in turn, increase the desire to contribute, first, and share knowledge afterwards, or after perceiving this support, to share knowledge directly. Researchers can reproduce and extend the current research to better understand and generalize actual findings, based on the experiences obtained.

(Wang et al. 2019) has been provided with empirical support to relate employee satisfaction, knowledge sharing, creativity capacities and job performance to sustainable management of human capital. In addition, the author concludes that the relationship between work satisfaction, sharing of information and capacity for creativity might have important moderating effects in different organizational modes. Thus, these findings can be used in a variety of ways to enhance efficient human resources management in the sense of hospitality.

(Dhamija et al. 2019) looked at the relationship between job satisfaction and the work quality factor of bank employees (n. 1/4 300) and the major impact these concepts on socio-demographic features showing a separate contribution to the literature that survives. In this study 5 private sector banks were considered in India and the primary data collection was performed using MST. The findings indicate a variance in job satisfaction ($R2$ 61.40%) as explained by efficiency of work-life buildings.

(Mahmood et al. 2019) explains how employee engagement through the mediating function of work satisfaction can be enhanced in the sense of particular HR variables, namely wages, job security and job enrichment. These show, in particular, the dedication of employees. The findings show that remuneration policies have a favorable relationship to employee happiness and engagement. With regard to the intermediate effect of job satisfaction, this study found that it mediates only between job satisfaction and the engagement of employees for non-monetary strategies.

The effect of recruitment & choice, training & development, performance evaluation, reimbursement & recompense on work satisfaction in the organisations has been described by **Bhawna Sareen (2018)**. The general findings of the present research suggest that the job satisfaction of workers employed in the company is affected by all undertaken variables including recruitment & selection, training & growth and performance assessments compensation & reward. This study also concludes that other organizations in various sectors that practice HR need to recognize increasing HRP affects employee satisfaction and can employ more HRP that is completely linked to the satisfaction of a safe working atmosphere.

(Ling et al. 2018) established HRM policies and procedures leading to more job satisfaction for PMs. The resu manifest that PMs who are contented with the HRM policies and work opportunities of their companies often have towering job satisfaction. Many HRM strategies are established which give rise to higher job satisfaction, e.g. a system for identifying and developing talent and taking appropriate steps to recognize and establish back in emergencies. Regrettably, certain policies are not applied to a large degree, including: consistently hiring an maintaining talented PMs, motivating PMs to prepare their careers, providing guidance for success and growth and employee appraisals.

(Anisimov et al. 2017) considered that human resource management is typically characterized as a mixture of behavior and choices to establish and execute a human resource management plan designed to meet the objecti of the company and build a competitive workforce. The lack of this approach leads to a negative team environment and a reduction in competitiveness.

(Nabi et al. 2017) analyzed the correlation between human resource management and job productivity motivation, training and growth, absenteeism and attrition, team work and employee engagement and compensation. The company is trying to create a connection between motivation and job efficiency. In this stu the author aims to link the success of the job to the satisfaction of workers and employees who are the key resources of the organization and the organization transforms the resources into assets and the assets are the lo term resources of the organization.

In integrating human resource management system (HRM) with work-related attitudes, **(Korff et al. 2017)** illustrated the position of the employee's future time perspective. We conclude that HRM systems have an indi effect on the person level of job satisfaction and adaptive institutional involvement as expressed by FTP based mutual interaction theory, signaling theory and affective event theory. The results of this multi-level study, consisting of 913 employees of 76 business units, indicate that HRM systems I directly impact FTP and (ii) indirectly affect employment and the engagement of the FTP organization.

Ishita Nafisa Islam (2016) defined in the Architects' Understanding of HRM practices and their level of job satisfaction in the various companies. Respondents were asked about understanding and work satisfaction and human resource management activities in their companies. Data were evaluated using the mean rating, key component analysis. The results indicate that most of the respondents were pleased with their overall work, although they were less satisfied with their salary.

(Huang et al. 2016) looked at the connection between satisfaction, employment satisfaction and turnover (TI) JS' position in JTS-TI relations. To analyze the variables in JTS and JS, the principal component analysis was performed. Different types of analysis were used to test the connection between the JTS, JS and TI. JS found a mediated a notably negative connection between JTS and TI. In this study author also indicates that JS is relate positively to JTS but is negatively linked to TI, which is consistent with what was stated in earlier studies.

(Mishra et al. 2016) applied human resource predictive analysis (HRPA) to get the optimized performance including the aim to generate improved return on investment for industries by decision making on the basis of data collection, metrices of human resources and predictive models. HRPA has mainly depends on three aspect such as; (i) need, (ii) approach with application and (iii) impact. Due to usefulness of HRPA in various areas it is required in HRM and it also helpful for organizations to gather HR-related costs while taking care of enhanced business performance including the employee as well as its satisfaction. Because of its rapidly changing behaviour and growing techniques it leads to accomplish 100% of accuracy for decision making in HR.

2.1 GREEN HUMAN RESOURCE MANAGEMENT

(Yong et al. 2020) explored the effects of green HRM on its sustainability through a cross-sectional analysis of 112 Malaysian manufacturing companies. Green recruitment and hiring has significant positive impact on sustainability. Despite initiatives such as green study, work description, green selection, green performance assessment and green rewards, sustainability has little or no effect. This study mainly focused on emerging economies with unique small Malaysian variables.

(Roscoe et al. 2019) demonstrated the connection between GHRM practices, green organizational culture enablers and the environmental accomplaishment of a company. In this author conducted a study of 204 employees at Chinese manufacturing Organization. Our results indicate that pro-environmental HRM activities including recruiting, training, assessment and motivation help the creation of green organizational culture enablers. This research contributes to the HRM theory in terms of originality and study usefulness by demonstrating that green organizational culture enablers positively mediate the relationship between GHRM activities and environmental performance.

(Stahl et al. 2020) Developed a multidimensional approach to sustainable HRM with a multidimensional purpose, including practices aimed at preventing negative effects with stakeholders and leading to positive triple-line outcomes such as citizens, the earth and prosperity. This sustainable HRM suggested here has more revolutionary and questions the majority on the interface with the wider issues facing society, the commitment of HRM to addressing the needs of a wide variety of stakeholders, including those outside the organization.

(Cogin et al. 2016) discussed the impact HRM has on healthcare staff working attitudes and hospital operational efficiency. Authors have considered behavioral management to be the most significant method of regulation used to monitor patients, allied health workers and junior doctors. Although hospitals use guidelines to promote compliance with existing policies, the ability of health care administrators to inspire and involve their staff has been hampered by overuse and often improper use of behavioral controls.

Table 2.1 Discussion of Existing Work

S. No.	Author Details and Reference	Aim of Study	Techniques Used	Obtained Outcomes
1.	(Jain et al. 2020)	Presented an approach to estimate if an person will leave the job or not. To analyze the effectiveness of employee appraisal along with rates of satisfaction in company which help into minimize the employee's rate of attrition	In this work the department with 1000 employees have been selected as a dataset on which the binary classifiers such as SVM, DT, and random forest RF have been Applied.	As per the final outcome it has to be observed that enhanced accuracy (99%) has been produced by RF which helps in prediction of employees that would likely leave the company
2.	(Ballal et al. 2020)	Employed various approaches adopted by researchers for predicting the rate of depletion of employees, in addition to an abstract view of the system to be implemented to forecast the rate of reduction of employees using Machine	From various machine learning (ML) techniques RF has been utilized for classification purpose.	This research discussed the performance of various classification algorithms, such as logistic regression (LR), SVM, KNN and Random Forests (RF), to estimate the likelihood of any employee leaving the organization.

		Learning (ML) approach, which performs well in the case of prediction of employees likely leaving the organization.		
3.	(Kakulapati et al. 2020)	Presented a machine learning (ML) approach to analyze the performance of employees along with the aim to predict the information about sections and department with lack of employees and requires taking employees.	By utilizing the K-means clustering approach to identify how many classes we will need to decide the characteristics that the HR will add to the new candidates or to promote the current candidates based on dependent features. Here by utilizing random forest (RF) to evaluate the knowledge of the employees to strengthen their role within the organization.	This research discusses about the remuneration and work performance information from different income groups.

4.	(Fernandes et al. 2019)	Built a method to forecast student success at the end of each year. To do this, a descriptive statistical analysis is used. The first dataset consists of variables gathered before the beginning of the previous year and the second dataset consists of academic variables gathered two months after school.	Selected gradient boosting machine (GBM) since it brings out a predictive models in the form of decision trees.	By utilizing the boosting approach of machine learning the accuracy has been improved since having a flexible nonlinear regression models which observed as helpful to boost the performance by consequently utilizing weak classification algorithms to incrementally changing data.

5.	Gordini et al. 2017)	Presented an approach to predict the amount of customers that stopped using the specific company's product in certain time limit in any business to business (B2B) organization of e-commerce.	Various supervised and unsupervised machine learning techniques have utilized for prediction such as support vector machines (SVM), neural network (NN) and logistic regression (LR) in which SVM is based on AUC parameter-selection scheme (SVMauc). As per this study, the procedure of parameter optimization plays a key role for prediction purpose as well as SVMauc performs better when applied on noisy, imbalance and non-linear marketing data.	The procedure of parameter optimization plays a key role for prediction purpose as well as SVMauc performs better when applied on noisy, imbalance and non-linear marketing data. The overall performance of SVM has seen as also enhanced as contrast to other techniques as it has accuracy of 89.67% which has increased by 4.57% and 5.87% against NN and LR correspondingly.
6.	(Kouziokas et al. 2017)	Developed a prediction model for high crime risk in certain areas. To get the regions with improved concentration of crime incidents i.e. clusters, spatial analysis has been utilized. To enhance the quality of transportation services as well as o ensure about the transportation safety in public areas is the key objective of this work.	Artificial neural networks (ANN) has been used here for prediction of values related to crime data.	The performance has been measured by using Mean Squared Error (MSE) by computing the prediction error. As it has cleared from the obtained outcome ANN produced enhanced prediction accuracy along with high crime risk. That considered as one of the fastest learning mechanism than backpropagation learning algorithms.
7.	(Gabriel et al. 2016)	Study the system perspective on HR and create a model that highlights how HR activities apply to three broad areas of HR: skills, motivation and opportunities-should improve emotional efficiency by enhancing the motivation and willingness of service staff to participate in intra-personal and/or inter-personal emotional	N/A	It reformulated a stand-alone view of HR practices and presented a model that showed how different HR practices contribute to each other's emotional performance, which in turn could impact customer service. Based on strategic HR literature, an integrative skill-enhancing HR activity model has been developed

		regulation.		that focuses on emotional job skills and promotes and encourages HR practices to influence, influence and influence HR practices.
8	(Paillé et al. 2014)	The purpose of this study is to explore the link between HRM and EM by highlighting how employees are helping their companies become greener at their own level.	Suggested the mechanism for mediating environmental citizenship organizational behavior (OCBE) and moderating the impact of environmental orientation.	This work particularly dealt with the relationship between SHRM and environmental efficiency from the employees' point of view.
9	(Pan et al. 2017)	Developed the prediction approach for earlier evaluation of difficulties to birth among pregnant women by consuming the 6457 datasets from Illinois department of human services of certain time interval i.e. from July 2014 to May 2015.	To produce the better prediction value of difficulties in birth using positive predictive value as the metric for selection selected (ML) algorithms such as (RF), (LDA), (LR) with L_2 penalty and naive Bayes (NB).	To measure the performance of different artificial intelligence (AI) based utilized technique, positive predictive value (PPV) has the metric. LR the top performer by producing an average PPV of 0.319. LDA of 0.317, RF of 0.301, and NB of 0.292.
10	(Kramar, R. (2014)	Investigated the key features of S (strategic) - HRM, some of its sustainability meanings and the relationship between sustainability and HRM. This then provides a description of the most significant aspects of sustainable HRM. While there is a range of views on sustainable HRM, this approach has many characteristics that distinguish it from SHRM.	N/A	It recognizes organizational results which are broader than financial results. Moreover, the negative and positive effects of HRM on a number of stakeholders are clearly identified; more attention is paid to the processes associated with the implementation of HRM policy and appreciation of the difficulty in reconciling successful organizational requirements.
11	Jeet et al. (2014)	Reflected an effort to inspect the effect of human resource management activities on employee satisfaction in the private sector. The approximate regression model found in the study that HRM activities such as	N/A	Recommended that HDFC Bank develop new policies to improve employee participation at mid-level and senior management levels. To achieve a greater level of job satisfaction, other

		preparation, assessment of results, teamwork and remuneration have a major effect on job satisfaction.		practices such as training, performance appraisal, teamwork and compensation has required.
12	(Cania, L. (2014)	Focused on the effect of human resources strategic management on its organizational success attainment. Discussed number many companies do the success metrics look competitive in the market along with importance of human resource management (HRM) to achieve organisation's success.	N/A	Organizational efficiency has changed by proactive resource management of individuals. It helps the achievement of goals for organizational efficiency. This also makes this possible for the company to be successful. HRM is a very important tool that ensures the organisation's continuity.
13	(Atteya, N. M. (2012)	The goal is to extend previous research by offering and testing an integrative model that explores the mediating variables that underlie the association between human resource management activities and job efficiency. Data was collected from 549 Petroleum Supervisors in Egypt.	N/A	According to the results obtained, human resource strategies have an indirect effect on work performance by: (a) positive job satisfaction, organizational engagement and organizational citizenship behavior, and (b) negative termination intentions and negative terms.
14.	(Shanmugam et al. 2019)	Aimed to compute the fear of job security in IT companies of Chennai. The authors consider several points and also applied machine learning for the implication of the same.	K-Means	The authors applied machine learning oriented K-means to divide the data into multiple groups namely unsatisfied, satisfied and others. This work inspires the proposed work as well.

CHAPTER 3. RESEARCH GAP & PROBLEM FORMULATION

- Majority sectors had their own specific strategy to be followed by employee and did not have any human resource strategy that lead to low level of job satisfaction
- Earlier research did not include the similarity and effectiveness of factors of risk handling, managerial ability and it having not ability to measure the ability of employee as well as performance analysis.
- Many research papers have focused on only four behavioural attributes such as leadership emphasis, message credibility, peer involvement, and employee empowerment to analyze the job satisfaction level of employee.

The use of Artificial Intelligence in HRM will revolutionize the working style and smooth running of the department as there is no better human and machine-based intelligence meeting place than our human resources department.

The technology will help transform HR department's daily recruiting, assessment, on boarding and management practices. On the other hand Artificial Intelligence is immune to typical conventional thinking that impacts candidate's race, gender or ethnicity on applicants screening. AI software can develop interview questions that disregard the history of the candidate and put more focus on their professional skill for a specific position.

The interview Questionnaires will be based upon candidate's previous working experience and the job for which they have applied, automation by AI helps filtering out superb candidates from the merely great. AI also helps relieve HR professionals from work of going through terabytes of data that includes candidates resume, social media accounts, reference letters and other sources.

This is a very hectic process covered by HR managers and they tend to cut through the data to get their job done in time, due to this negligence loop holes appear in the company's recruiting process. This further leads to hiring people that are not fit for the company resulting in further re- hiring procedures which costs company both time and money. AI can include after hiring performance assessment which will show deep insight into employee's capabilities and potential. AI also helps with HR management by monitoring employee's performance through various performance metrics.It also helps in setting up grading systems for each employee and automatic review system in accordance with the set performance goals.

3.1 OBJECTIVES

1. To Manage the data through HR data Analytics

2. To Develop an algorithm for human capital analysis through machine learning

3. To Develop technique for forecasting in human resource planning

4. To compare the developed system with the state of art technique

CHAPTER 4 PROPOSED WORK

The main focus of this exploration work is determining the level of satisfaction of employees in various working areas such as Technical, IT, sales, marketing, accounting, and production companies (Delaney et al. 1996). The word job satisfaction is a dynamic and important definition for human resource management (HRM) to better understand that most workers do not feel that their work is being adequately compensated. They also don't agree that certain organizations are doing well to promote, train or handle high quality performance in an efficient manner. (Becker et al. 1996), (Truss et al. 2001).There are various dimensions that are available for job satisfaction some commonly noticed are; satisfaction with work itself, wages, relation with supervisor and co-workers including the opportunities for advancement. Each aspect applies to the general satisfaction of employee's with job , although different people define jobs in different way (Boselie et al. 2005), (Selvarajan et al. 2007), (Zhao, Xin(2008)).

Specifically job satisfaction is one of measuring strategy to analyze the effectiveness of employees to get the productivity through employees by taking into account the current state of work. (Mishra et al. 2016)

4.1 Proposed work for Developing for human capital analysis

- Dataset used

- For work simulation of proposed approach, we consumed HRA- Dataset from the Kaggle repository t the good insights of a problem that is faced by human resource of any department of any company.

- The dataset contains employee profiles of a large company, where each record is an employee.

- The dataset describe the satisfaction level is around 60% and the performance average is around 70% see that on average people work on 3 to 4 projects a year and about 200 hours per months.

Table 4.1 Dataset

Name of Variables	Explanation
satisfaction_level	Denotes the job satisfaction level of employees
last_evaluation	Final evaluated values
number_project	Total number of projects
average_montly_hours	Average hours of every month
time_spend_company	Total time spend at the company
Work_accident	Whether the employees have any work accident
Left	Whether the employees has left from work
promotion_last_5years	Whether employees got a promotion in last 5 years.
Sales	Respect to the job in sale department
Salary	Amount of paid to employees

4.1.1 Algorithm for Proposed Work

Required Input:	Feature Set (FS)← Extracted feature from Pre-processed data
	Fitness Function ←Designed fitness function for feature selection
	C←Target/Category in terms of employee parameters (High, Medium and Low)
	N←Number of Neurons
Obtained Output:	Net ← Trained structure

1 **Start**
2 **Load Dataset,** Feature Data (FS)
3 **To optimized the FS, apply GA**
4 **Set up basic operators of GA:** Population Size (P) – Based on the number of properties
        CO – Crossover Operators
        Mu – Mutation Operators
                          OFS – Optimized Feature Set
  Fitness Function:
                  {

Where cvx is the current selected attribute value, mutation rate is random and the crossover is the average of all selected rows for the same attribute value. R= Length (FS) //Calculate the Length of FSin terms of R

5 Calculate Length of FS in terms of R
6 Set, Optimized Feature S, OFS = []
7 **For i in rang of R**
8   $F_s = FS(i) =$
9   $F_t = \Sigma$
10
11 Nvar = Number of variables
12 $Best_{Prop}$ = OFS = GA (F(f), T, Nvar, Set up of GA)
13 **End – For**
14 Consider, T-Data = OFS //Pass optimized feature set as input data to ANN.
15 **Initialize the basic parameters of ANN for OFS** like N, Epochs, performances, technique used, and data division.
16 **For i = 1 → T-Data**
17   **If T-Data> High Category**
18   Group (1) = Features (OFS)
19   **Else if Medium >T-Data<High Category**
20   Group (2) = Features (OFS)
21   **Else belong to Low Category**

22 Group (3) = Features (OFS)
23 End – If
24 End – For
25 **Initialized the ANN using Training data and Group**
26 Net = Newff ( )
27 **Set the training parameters according to the requirements and train the system**
28 **Net = Train (Net, T-Data, Group)**
29 **Return:** Net as a trained structure
30 **End – Function**

4.1.2 Algorithm: Optimized feature using GA

Required Input:	Feature Set (FS) ← Extracted feature from Pre-processed data
	Fitness Function ← Designed fitness function for feature selection
Obtained Output:	OFS ← Optimized Feature set

1 **Start**
2 **Load Dataset,** Feature Data (FS)
3 **Apply GA, To optimized the FS**
4 **Set up basic operators of GA:** Population Size (P) – Based on the number of properties
                      Cr // Crossover Operators
                      Mu // Mutation Operators
                      OFS // Optimized Feature Set
        Fitness Function:
        Mutation Type: Linear
        Cross-over=Intermediate
            {

Where cvx is the current selected attribute value, mutation rate is linear and the crossover is the average of all selected rows for the same attribute value. R= Length (FS) //Calculate the Length of FS in terms of R

5 **Set, OFS = [ ]** // Optimized Feature
6 **For i= 1 to R**
7   F_s = FS (i) =
8    $F_s = \Sigma$
9
10 N_{var} // Number of variables
11 $Best_{Prop}$ = OFS = GA (F(f), T, Nvar, Set up of GA)

12 End(For)

4.2 Experimental setup

USED PLATFORM

The results were obtained after the simulation of the code in platform of Python. The detailed explanation of this environment is provided below;

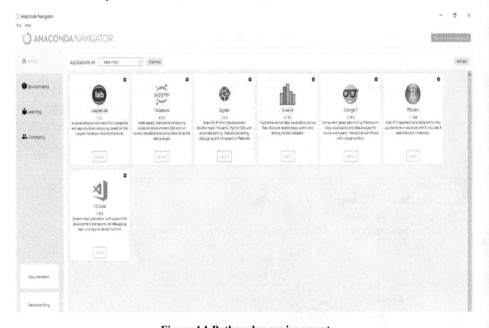

Figure 4.1 Python dev environment

In **figure 4.1** shows the python dev environment i.e. Anaconda navigator also known as desktop GUI that helps to process applications and easily manage packages.

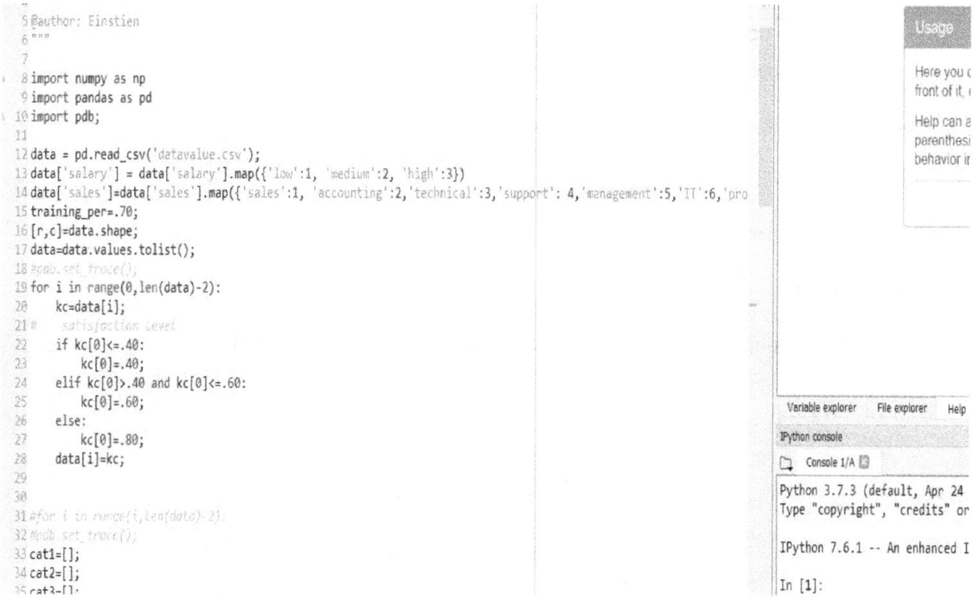

```
 5 @author: Einstien
 6 """
 7
 8 import numpy as np
 9 import pandas as pd
10 import pdb;
11
12 data = pd.read_csv('datavalue.csv');
13 data['salary'] = data['salary'].map({'low':1, 'medium':2, 'high':3})
14 data['sales']=data['sales'].map({'sales':1, 'accounting':2,'technical':3,'support': 4,'management':5,'IT':6,'pro
15 training_per=.70;
16 [r,c]=data.shape;
17 data=data.values.tolist();
18 #pdb.set_trace();
19 for i in range(0,len(data)-2):
20     kc=data[i];
21 #    satisfaction level
22     if kc[0]<=.40:
23         kc[0]=.40;
24     elif kc[0]>.40 and kc[0]<=.60:
25         kc[0]=.60;
26     else:
27         kc[0]=.80;
28     data[i]=kc;
29
30
31 #for i in range(i,len(data)-2):
32 #pdb.set_trace();
33 cat1=[];
34 cat2=[];
35 cat3=[];
```

Figure 4.2 Spyder code unit

To execute the task of presented approach, a very powerful scientific environment of Python known as spyder and the coding unit is given in **figure 4.2** which designed for researchers.

- GA will be used for row selection

- Fitness function – Every attribute is passed through it with linear mutation value, random mutation rate and crossover value is obtained.

- If attribute satisfies the fitness function the attribute value is changed from 0 to 1.

- If count of 1's is greater than that of 0's it means most of the attributes are considered for generating satisfaction level

Category wise bifurcation

- Satisfaction level of employees is considered as a judgment class.
- Satisfaction level is categorized s in 3 categories to measure level.
- LOW
- MEDIUM
- HIGH
- Satisfaction level lies between 0.09 to 0.90

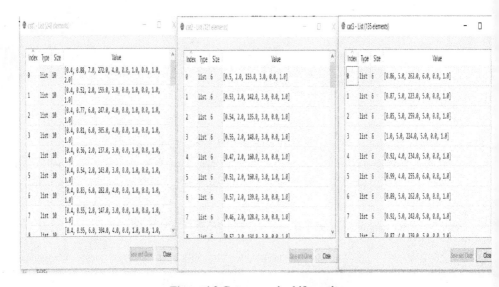

Figure 4.3 Category wise bifurcation

In **figure 4.3** shows the distinct category wise bifurcation of collected dataset. Basically the term bifurcation is corresponding to the point or area at which something divides into specified categories or parts. **In this work the large amount of collected datasets is partitioned among some categories** to measure the level of satisfaction on the basis of salary, last evaluation and list of projects etc. After get the categorized value of large data it needs to be optimized to get the relevant information. For this purpose in our approach GA is utilized as an optimizer and the category of data is updated.

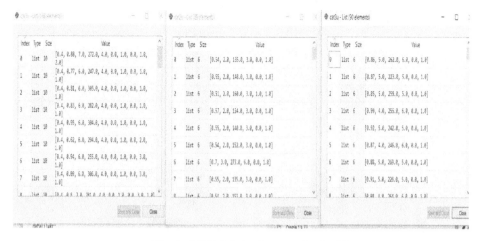

Figure 4.4 Updated category value by GA

After get the categorized value of large data it needs to be optimized to get the relevant information. For this purpose in our approach GA is utilized as an optimizer and the category of data is updated as shown in **figure 4.4**

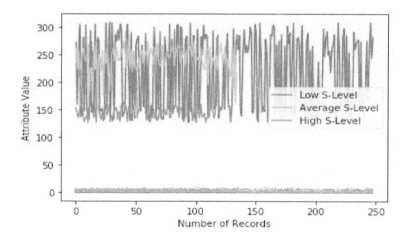

Figure 4.5 Scale Value

The satisfaction level of employees through categorizing it into three level of satisfaction i.e. low S (satisfaction) - level, average S (satisfaction) - level and high S (satisfaction)- level. In **figure 4.5**

43

represent the scale value of these three satisfaction level by three different colors such as green, orange and blue corresponding to high S – level, average S – level and low S – level. The graph of attribute level is plotted against number of record along x-axis and along y-axis different attribute value of satisfaction level is given.

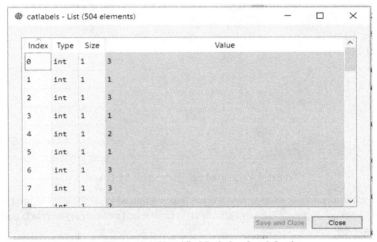

Figure 4.6 Classified Labels of satisfaction

The dataset after bifurcation and updated by GA is assigned by the labels in **figure 4.6**

satisfactio	last_evalu.	number_p	average_n	time_spen	Work_acci	left	promotion	sales	salary
0.38	0.53	2	157	3	0	1	0	sales	low
0.8	0.86	5	262	6	0	1	0	sales	medium
0.11	0.88	7	272	4	0	1	0	sales	medium
0.72	0.87	5	223	5	0	1	0	sales	low
0.37	0.52	2	159	3	0	1	0	sales	low
0.41	0.5	2	153	3	0	1	0	sales	low
0.1	0.77	6	247	4	0	1	0	sales	low
0.92	0.85	5	259	5	0	1	0	sales	low
0.89	1	5	224	5	0	1	0	sales	low
0.42	0.53	2	142	3	0	1	0	sales	low
0.45	0.54	2	135	3	0	1	0	sales	low
0.11	0.81	6	305	4	0	1	0	sales	low
0.84	0.92	4	234	5	0	1	0	sales	low
0.41	0.55	2	148	3	0	1	0	sales	low
0.36	0.56	2	137	3	0	1	0	sales	low
0.38	0.54	2	143	3	0	1	0	sales	low
0.45	0.47	2	160	3	0	1	0	sales	low
0.78	0.99	4	255	6	0	1	0	sales	low
0.45	0.51	2	160	3	1	1	1	sales	low
0.76	0.89	5	262	5	0	1	0	sales	low

Figure 4.7 Selected attributes retrieved after GA

4.3 Proposed work for Forecasting in Human Resource Planning

STEP-1 Upload the HRA dataset to perform the work simulation of the model by using excel read command and transform the data in terms of numeric data for further processing.

STEP-2 Before started the processing on uploaded datasets, we have to apply pre-processing on the datasets to produce a compatible data. To get the enhanced prediction accuracy of presented approach, we requires to understand the challenge that will helpful for selecting the accurate approach of the data optimization and Artificial Intelligence (AI) technology to produce the best predictions. We apply pre-processing on the data to change the string data in terms of numeric data for fast computation purpose and we change the name of ‒salesǀ by ‒Name of Departmentǀ and ‒salaryǀ by ‒low, medium and high.

STEP-3 After that, we analyze the data on the basis of three different analysis queries such as:

- Total number of employees in each department.
- Total number of employees as per the range of salary i.e. low, medium and high.
- Total number of employees on the basis of defined range of salary and department.

STEP-4 After analysis of the pre-processed data on the basis of above question some important extracted features are obtained as;

- Level of Satisfaction including final evaluation.
- Monthly hours in average and total number of projects.
- Older employees including more than 10 years in company

STEP-5 To predict the level of satisfaction for employees, the evaluation of correlation is very useful statistical analysis. So we determine the correlation among two variables in the dataset.

- Compute -VE correlation among satisfaction_level and the employees that left the company.
- Compute +VE correlation among total number of projects and hours of months in average.
- Compute Last_evaluation correlation by using the number_project and average_monthly_hours.

- Computation of Low –VE correlation among Work_accident and employees who left the company.

STEP-6 Determine the hypothesis of the presented approaches below;

- HYPOTHESIS 1- Salary is one of the reasons for employees to leave the company.
- HYPOTHESIS 2- Working environment is one of the reasons to quit the job.

STEP-7 According to this hypothesis, the computation of features is done in terms of the Total count, mean, standard deviation, minimum, maximum value on the basis of attributes the such as satisfaction level, last evaluation, number project, average monthly hours, time spend company, Work accident, left, promotion in the last 5years, sales and salary.

STEP-8 Apply Genetic Algorithm (GA) as an optimizer to select the optimal set of features from the features available in dataset to improve the quality of features on the basis of fitness evaluation. So, we implemented a novel fitness function to select the optimal feature sets through utilizing the concept of GA.

4.3.1 ARTIFICIAL NEURAL NETWORK (ANN)

The approach of AI gives optimum level of interactions among users and computers. It aims to construct a computer syst that simulates human thought and its shared influences (Coelho et al. 2019). Ideally, in the application of AI requires la amount of storage capacity, thinking logic of human and the abilities of contextual analysis. The system uses AI to descr the job features for identification of human resources. In the ANN branch of AI that designed for simulating the process human learning. Although the general structure is very easy making very complex relationship learning easy (Berhil e 2020). It can improve a talent selection strategy by supplying ANN with successful and ineffective recruitment data. Another branch of AI is a knowledge system that combines one field of expertise to create one Skill Bank and simulates judgment of human experts . The expert system can be implemented for distinct activities of training, staffing etc. Anoth point of consideration is that not every problem can be sought through an intelligence system.
The neural network is sort of a system that simulates the cranial nerve cell operations of a creature (Čerka et al. 2017). Although it is not quite similar being focused on "experiencing" or conceptual behavior. In the realistic world, the neural network can recognise, assess and notice all the phenomena. The neural network uses a simple basic framework: the processing part, the layer and the network to form a cognitive and predictive system. While facing dynamic and non-line challenges , there are also some conditions that people cannot manage (Buchanan et al. 2005).

The term intelligence (specifically artificial) generates the experience as per the past events to produce certain expectatio regarding futures. The intermediate in between the experience and expectations is the sense. Such kind of combinations l numeric weights which can be tuned on the basis of past experience producing neural networks (NN) adaptive as inputs ability to learn (Waterman et al. 1971). ANN is connected to the analytic modelling since in human brains cognitive appear from the occupation performed by neural networks that convey information from one region of cerebrum to anoth Training in NNs is tends to the selection of one model from the collection of allowed which reduces the criterion of cost. Supervised learning approach is considerably a leaning mechanism from a guide in the shape of functionality that provid response on the quality of solution in continuous manner.

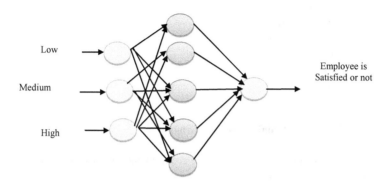

Figure 0.8 Training Process of Neural Network

In reality, the network that runs a neural network will obtain higher cognitive metrics by adding one or more hidden units.(Wirtz et al. 2019).

In normal situations, ANN consists of a single layer and a layer in which each layer has a specific number of neurons and the hidden units (one or more). The input signal transfers the NN from the input level to the exit level through the secret level in the feedforward neural network (FFNN).**(Kouziokas et al. 2017) (Sanger, T. D. (1989))**

4.3.1a Algorithm: Predict Satisfaction level using ANN

Required Input:	OFS←Pass optimized feature Set as input data to ANN. **It contains the attribute sets from the dataset if the entire row is selected by Genetic Algorithm. As for example, it there are total 500 rows in satisfied category with 8 attributes from dataset, 500*8 is the size out of which if 80 rows are not selected, then 420*8 with group label 1 will be passed to Neural network as an input.**
	C←Target/Category in terms of employee parameters, It is the class labels, in the proposed case, there are three class labels for non-satisfied, moderate-satisfied and satisfied.
	N←Number of Neurons- (15)
Obtained Output:	Net ← Trained structure(This structure will contain the propagated weights through Neural Training)

1 **Start Prediction**
2 Load Training Data, P-Data = **OFS**
3 **Start the basic parameters of ANN** like N (Number of Neurons), Epochs, performances, technique

used, and data division.
4 **For i = 1 → T-Data**
5 **If T-Data> High Category**
6 Group (1) = Features (OFS)
7 **Else if Medium >T-Data<High Category**
8 Group (2) = Features (OFS)
9 **Else belong to Low Category**
10 Group (3) = Features (OFS)
11 **End – If**
12 **End – For**
13 **Initialize ANN utilizing Training data and Group**
14 **Net = Newff ( )**
15 **Set the training parameters according to the requirements and train the system**
16 **Net = Train (Net, T-Data, Group)**
17 **Return:** Net as a trained structure
End – Function

4.3.2 EXPERIMENTAL SET UP

- It contains the attribute sets from the dataset if the entire row is selected by Genetic Algorithm.

- As for example, it there are total 500 rows in satisfied category with 8 attributes from dataset, 500*8 is the size out of which if 80 rows are not selected, then 420*8 with group label 1 will be passed to Neural network as an input.

- Feed forward neural network is used to form a training model

- It is the class labels, in the proposed case, there are three class labels for non-satisfied, moderate-satisfied and satisfied.

- This structure will contain the propagated weights through Neural Training)

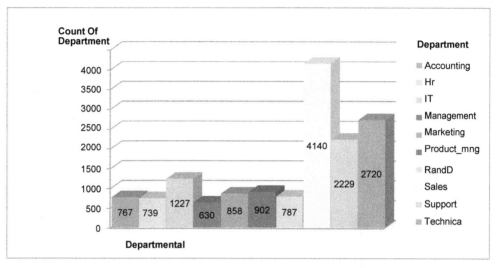

Fig 4.9 Total number of employees in each department

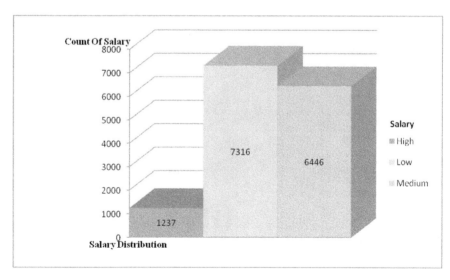

Fig 4.10 Total number of employees as per the range of salary i.e. low, medium and high

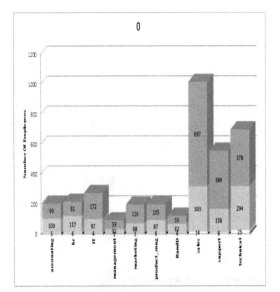
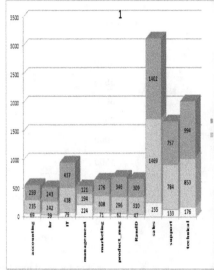

Fig 4.11 Total number of employees on the basis of defined range of salary and department

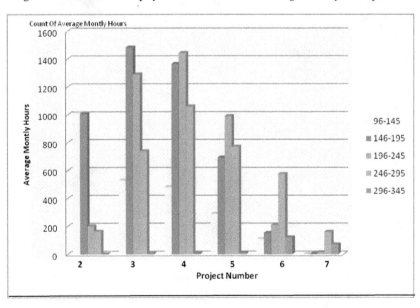

Fig 4.12 Monthly hours in average and total number of projects

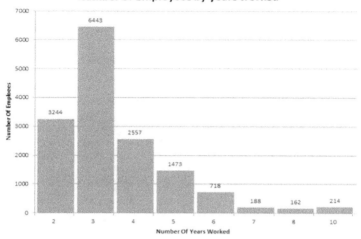

Fig 4.13 Older employees including more than 10 years in company

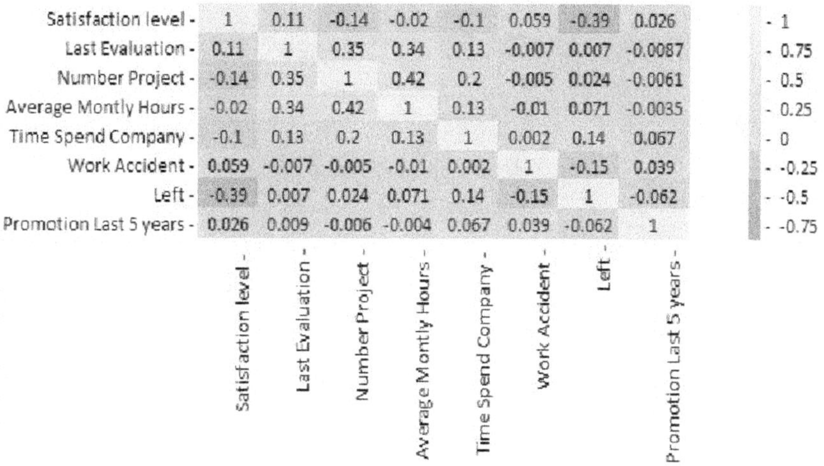

	Satisfaction level	Last Evaluation	Number Project	Average Montly Hours	Time Spend Company	Work Accident	Left	Promotion Last 5 years	
Satisfaction level -	1	0.11	-0.14	-0.02	-0.1	0.059	-0.39	0.026	- 1
Last Evaluation -	0.11	1	0.35	0.34	0.13	-0.007	0.007	-0.0087	- 0.75
Number Project -	-0.14	0.35	1	0.42	0.2	-0.005	0.024	-0.0061	- 0.5
Average Montly Hours -	-0.02	0.34	0.42	1	0.13	-0.01	0.071	-0.0035	- 0.25
Time Spend Company -	-0.1	0.13	0.2	0.13	1	0.002	0.14	0.067	- 0
Work Accident -	0.059	-0.007	-0.005	-0.01	0.002	1	-0.15	0.039	- -0.25
Left -	-0.39	0.007	0.024	0.071	0.14	-0.15	1	-0.062	- -0.5
Promotion Last 5 years -	0.026	0.009	-0.006	-0.004	0.067	0.039	-0.062	1	- -0.75

Fig 4.14 Evaluation of correlation

CHAPTER 5 RESULT AND ANALYSIS

RESULT AND ANALYSIS

To measure the performance of presented approach along with compare and analyse various Parameters, such as Precision, Recall, F-measure are measured to achieve the outcome. The mathematical expressions of the Parameters are shown below:

5.1 COMPARATIVE ANALYSIS

$$Precision = \frac{True_{positive}}{True_{positive} + False_{positive}}$$

$$Recall = \frac{True_{positive}}{True_{positive} + True_{negative}}$$

$$F - measure = \frac{2 * Precision * Recall}{Precision + Recall}$$

To test the performance of the system to detect the employee's satisfaction level, a set of experiments have been performed on the dataset. The experiment uses 70 percent of the data to practice, while the other 30% to test the system's efficiency. The demonstartions have been performed for multiple iterations.

5.1.1 Computed parameters for 400 Elements

The desire of this work is to inspect the satisfaction level of workers in the company by considering different factors, as mentioned above. This segment describes the performance of the said work in terms of precision, recall, and F-measure for 400 Elements.

5.1.1.1 Precision for 400 Elements

Table 5.1 Precision for 400 Elements

Number of iterations	GA	ANN	GA-ANN
10	88.98	90.78	97.85
20	88.76	90.67	97.56
30	88.45	89.88	97
40	87.66	89.98	96.66
50	87.78	89.33	96.76
60	87.32	89.09	95.98

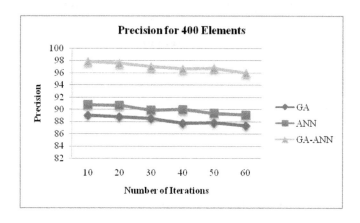

Figure 5.1 Precision for 400 Elements

The parameter precision implies that two or more measurement values are closed to each other. Figure 5.1 shows the comparison between the proposed hybrid GA-ANN, GA and ANN. The precision value for the proposed GA-ANN lies between 98 to 95, as the iteration increases from 10 to 60 on the other hand the precision value for GA 91 to 89 and in case of ANN 89 to 87, which show that the proposed GA-ANN performed well as compare to GA and ANN.

This is because using GA with ANN, ANN is optimized or taught with greater accuracy because the best information is given to ANN.

5.1.1.2 Recall for 400 Elements

Table 5.2 Recall for 400 elements

Number of iterations	GA	ANN	GA-ANN
10	88.76	90.66	97.78
20	88.65	90.56	97.44
30	88.34	89.76	96.88
40	87.78	89.54	96.45
50	87.67	88.87	95.88
60	87.32	88.70	95.66

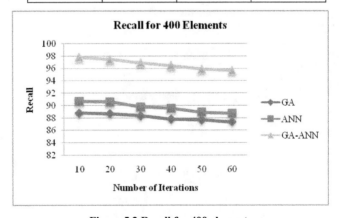

Figure 5.2 Recall for 400 elements

The parameter, Recall is defined as the how many of the true positives have been obtained found. The **figure 5.2** shows the comparison between the propose work (GA-ANN), GA and ANN in terms of Recall for the 400 elements. The maximum value for the proposed work is 97 and whereas in case of GA it is 88 and for the ANN it is 90 that show that the proposed work perform well as compare to GA and ANN. The results show that using proposed GA with ANN approach, recall value is high, means that the GA-with ANN approach detects accurate employees either satisfied or not as per their performance evaluation parameters. The average value of GA is 88.08, ANN is 89.68 and GA with ANN is 96.68.

5.1.1.3 F-measure for 400 Elements

Table 5.3 F-measure for 400 Elements

Number of iterations	GA	ANN	GA-ANN
10	88.86	90.71	97.81
20	66.7	90.61	97.49
30	88.39	89.81	96.93
40	87.71	89.75	96.55
50	87.72	89.09	96.31
60	87.32	88.89	95.81

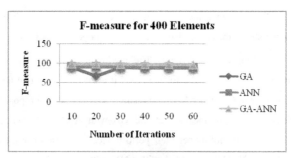

Figure 5.3 F-measure for 400 Elements

The term F-measure defined as a measure of accuracy of the work and it has been explained graphically in the **figure 5.3** The figure shows the comparison between GA, ANN and GA-ANN. The mean worth of GA is 84.45, ANN is 89.81 and GA-ANN is 96.81.This figure shows that proposed work gives better result than GA and ANN.This is because using GA with ANN, ANN is optimized or taught with greater accuracy because the best information is given to ANN.

5.1.2 Computed Parameters for 600 Elements

5.1.2.1 Precision for 600 elements

The desire of this work is to inspect the satisfaction level of workers in the company by considering different factors, as mentioned above. This segment describes the performance of the said work in terms of precision, recall, and F-measure for 600 Elements.

Table 5.4 Precision for 600 elements

Number of iterations	GA	ANN	GA-ANN
10	88.87	90.56	97.66
20	88.68	90.45	97.34
30	88.32	89.67	96.88
40	87.45	89.34	96.54
50	87.67	89.12	96.33
60	87.22	89.05	95.56

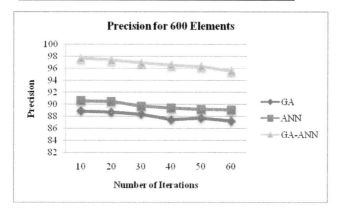

Figure 5.4 Precision for 600 elements

Figure 5.4 shows the precision comparison for 600 elements for Precision value. In case of 10th iteration, the precision value for proposed work is 97.7 where as for the same iteration the precision value for GA is 88.8 and for ANN is 90.5 that indicate the proposed work perform well as compare to other. The average value of GA is 88.03, ANN is 89.69 and GA with is 96.71.

5.1.2.2 Recall for 600 Elements

Table 5.5 Recall for 600 elements

Number of iterations	GA	ANN	GA-ANN
10	88.70	90.60	97.67
20	88.60	90.48	97.40
30	88.30	89.70	96.80
40	87.69	89.48	96.40
50	87.58	88.79	95.82
60	87.22	88.65	95.59

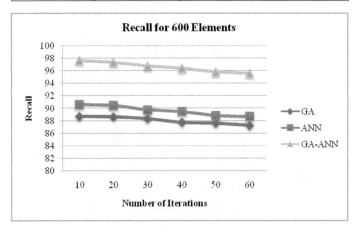

Figure 5.5 Recall for 600 elements

Figure 5.5 shows comparison between the proposed work (GA-ANN) and GA and ANN for the 600 element for Recall value. The maximum value for the proposed work (GA-ANN) is 97.6 for the 10th iteration, on the other side the Recall value for the GA is 88.7 and for ANN it is 90.6 that clearly shows that the proposed work perform well as compare to the other. The average value of GA is 88.01, ANN is 89.61 and GA with ANN is 96.61.

5.1.2.3 F-measure for 600 Elements

Table 5.6 F-measure for 600 Elements

Number of iterations	GA	ANN	GA-ANN
10	88.78	90.57	97.66
20	88.63	90.46	97.3
30	88.3	89.68	96.83
40	87.56	89.4	95.28
50	87.62	88.95	96.07
60	87.22	88.49	95.58

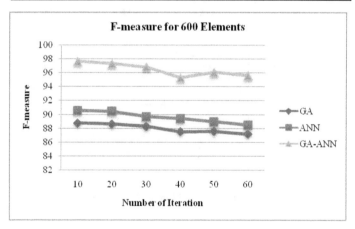

Figure 5.6 F-measure for 600 Elements

Figure 5.6 shows the comparison between GA, ANN and GA-ANN. In this figure x-axis potrays the Number of Iteration and Y-axis potrays the F-measure. The average value of GA is 88.01, ANN is 89.59 and GA-ANN is 96.45. The average value of GA is 88.01, ANN is 89.59 and GA with ANN is 96.45. The graph depicts our proposed work yields finer results in contrast to GA and ANN.

5.1.3 Computed Parameters for 800 elements

The desire of this work is to inspect the satisfaction level of workers in the company by considering different factors, as mentioned above. This segment describes the performance of the said work in terms of precision, recall, and F-measure 800 Elements.

5.1.3.1 Precision for 800 elements

Table 5.7 Precision for 800 elements

Number of iterations	GA	ANN	GA-ANN
10	88.77	90.43	97.54
20	88.64	90.35	97.20
30	88.29	89.56	96.76
40	87.40	89.29	96.43
50	87.60	89.07	96.28
60	87.20	89	95.48

Figure 5.7 Precision for 800 elements

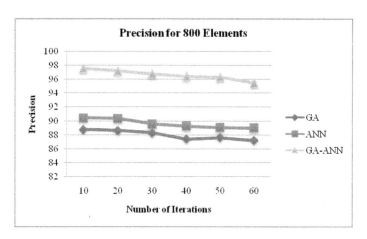

Figure 5.7 shows the precision comparison among proposed work, GA and ANN for 800 elements for Precision. When we compare the difference in precision value for the proposed work with GA and ANN in the 30th iteration we found that the value for the proposed work is 96.7 while in the case of GA it is 88.2 and in case of ANN it is 89.5 that show the performance difference among proposed work (GA-ANN) and GA, ANN.

5.1.3.2 Recall for 800 Elements

Table 5.8 Recall for 800 elements

Number of iterations	GA	ANN	GA-ANN
10	88.67	90.54	97.58
20	88.55	90.40	97.39
30	88.27	89.67	96.77
40	87.65	89.42	96.38
50	87.52	88.73	95.76
60	87.19	88.63	95.55

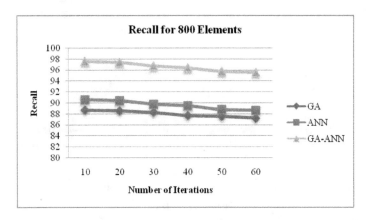

Figure 5.8 Recall for 800 elements

Figure 5.8 shows the Recall value comparison in case of proposed work, GA and ANN for 800 elements. When we compare the difference in Recall value for the proposed work with GA and ANN in the 30th iteration we found that the value for the proposed work is 97.5 while in the case of GA it is 88.6 and in case of ANN it is 90.5 that show the performance difference among proposed word (GA-ANN) and GA, ANN.

5.1.3.3 F-measure for 800 Elements

Table 5.9 F-measure for 800 Elements

Number of iterations	GA	ANN	GA-ANN
10	88.71	90.48	97.55
20	88.59	90.37	97.29
30	88.27	89.61	96.76
40	87.08	89.35	96.4
50	87.55	88.89	96.01
60	87.19	88.81	95.51

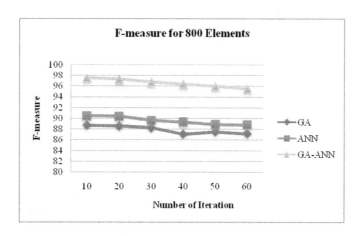

Figure 5.9 F-measure for 800 Elements

Figure 5.9 shows F-measure for 800 elements. In this figure the X-axis potrays the Number of Iterations and Y-axis potrays the F-measure. At iteration 20th the value of GA is 88.59, ANN is 90.37 and GA-ANN is 97.29. The average value of GA is 87.89, ANN is 89.58 and GA-ANN is 96.58. In all the iteration, it clearly indicates the Recall value proposed work performs well as compare to ANN and GA.

5.1.4 Computed Parameters for 1000 elements

The desire of this work is to inspect the satisfaction level of workers in the company by considering different factors, as mentioned above. This segment describes the performance of the said work in terms of precision, recall, and F-measure of 1000 Elements.

5.1.4.1 Precision for 1000 Elements

Table 5.10 Precision for 1000 elements

Number of iterations	GA	ANN	GA-ANN
10	88.72	90.40	97.49
20	88.60	90.30	97.17
30	88.21	89.50	96.66
40	87.38	89.22	96.40
50	87.56	89.03	96.22
60	87.16	89	95.43

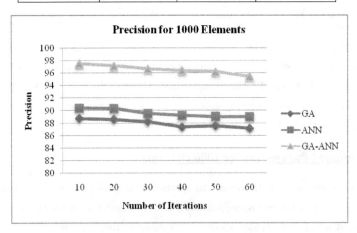

Figure 5.10 Precision for 1000 Elements

Figure 5.10 shows the comparison between the proposed work (GA-ANN) and GA and ANN for the 1000 element for Precision value. The maximum Precision value for the proposed work (GA- ANN) is 97.4 for the 10th iteration, on the other side the precision value for the GA is 88 and for ANN it is 90 that clearly shows that the proposed work performs better than other model.

5.1.4.2 Recall for 1000 Elements

Table 5.11 Recall for 1000 Elements

Number of iterations	GA	ANN	GA-ANN
10	88.60	90.49	97.45
20	88.50	90.35	97.33
30	88.22	89.60	96.66
40	87.55	89.38	96.29
50	87.48	88.69	95.70
60	87.10	88.58	95.50

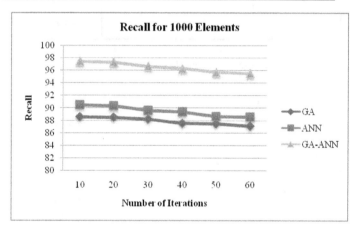

Figure 5.11 Recall for 1000 Elements

Figure 5.11 shows the difference in Recall value for 1000 element. For 40th iteration the recall value for the proposed work is 96.2 and for the sane iteration the recall value for GA is 87 and ANN is 89. In all the iteration, it clearly indicates the Recall value in proposed work performs well as compare to ANN and GA.

5.1.4.3 F-measure for 1000 Elements

Table 5.12 F-measure for 1000 Elements

Number of iterations	GA	ANN	GA-ANN
10	88.65	90.44	97.46
20	88.54	90.32	97.24
30	88.21	89.54	96.66
40	87.46	89.29	96.34
50	87.51	88.85	95.95
60	87.12	88.78	95.46

Figure 5.12 F-measure for 1000 Elements

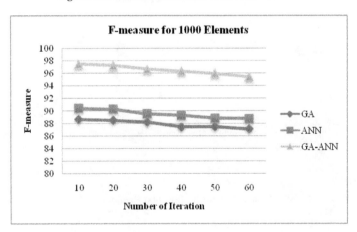

Figure 5.12 shows F-measure for 1000 elements. In this figure the X-axis potrays the Number of Iterations and Y-axis potrays the F-measure. At iteration 50th the value of GA is 87.51, ANN is 88.85 and GA-ANN is 95.95. The average value of GA is 87.91, ANN is 89.53 and GA-ANN is 96.51. In all the iteration, it clearly indicates the Recall value in proposed work performs well as compare to ANN and GA.

5.2 To compare the developed system with the state of art technique (COMPARISON OF GA WITH K-MEANS AND GA WITH ANN)

To show the effectiveness of the proposed (GA with ANN) approach, comparison with the existing approach that is with K-means as a machine learning approach has been shown.

5.2.1 Computed Parameters for 400 elements

The desire of this work is to inspect the satisfaction level of workers in the company by considering different factors, as mentioned above. This segment describes the performance of the said work in terms of precision, recall, and F-measure of 400 Elements.

5.2.1.1 Precision for 400 Elements

Table 5.13 Precision for 400 Elements

Number of iterations	GA with K-means	GA with ANN
10	96.89	97.85
20	96.76	97.56
30	96.54	97
40	95.67	96.66
50	95.45	96.76
60	94.98	95.98

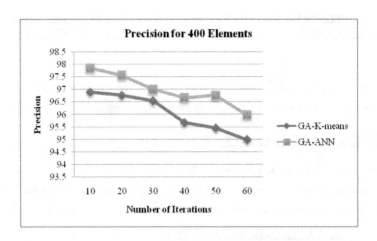

Figure 5.13 Precision for 400 Elements

Figure 5.13 shows the comparison between two techniques one is GA with K-means and another is GA with ANN for 400 elements. From the graph it is clear that the proposed approach executes well in contrast to other approach. Also, when the number of iterations escalate, the precision value drops. This might be due to the performance of the testing sample again and again, so that accurate value can be evaluated. The average value of GA-K- means is 95.04 and average value off GA-ANN is 96.96.

5.2.1.2 Recall for 400 Elements

Table 5.14 Recall for 400 Elements

Number of iterations	GA-K-means	GA-ANN
10	96.55	97.78
20	96.34	97.44
30	95.77	96.88
40	94.98	96.45
50	94.77	95.88
60	94.65	95.66

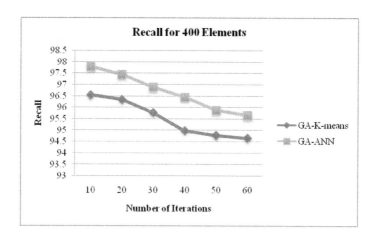

Figure 5.14 Recall for 400 Elements

Figure 5.14 represents the comparison of recall using GA with ANN and K-means as a machine learning approach. At iteration 20th the value of GA-K-means is 96.34 and GA-ANN is 97.44. The average value of GA-K-means is 95.51 and GA-ANN is 96.68.

5.2.1.3 F-measure for 400 Elements

Table 5.15 F-measure for 400 Elements

Number of iterations	GA-K-means	GA-ANN
10	96.71	97.81
20	96.54	97.49
30	96.15	96.93
40	96.32	96.55
50	95.1	96.31
60	94.81	95.81

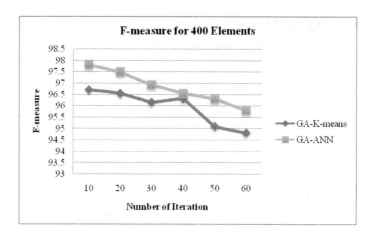

Figure 5.15 F-measure for 400 Elements

Figure 5.15 represents the comparison of F-measure using GA with ANN and K-means as a machine learning approach. At iteration 10th the value of GA-K-means is 96.71 and GA-ANN is 97.81. The mean worth of GA-K-means is 95.93 and the mean worth of GA-ANN is 96.81.

5.2.2 Computed Parameter for 600 elements

The desire of this work is to inspect the satisfaction level of workers in the company by considering different factors, as mentioned above. This segment describes the performance of the said work in terms of precision, recall, and F-measure for 600 Elements.

5.2.2.1 Precision for 600 Elements

Table 5.16 Precision for 600 Elements

Number of iterations	GA-K-means	GA-ANN
10	96.45	97.66
20	96.34	97.34
30	95.78	96.88
40	95.45	96.54
50	95	96.33
60	94.34	95.56

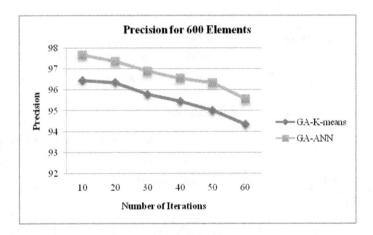

Figure 5.16 Precision for 600 Elements

Figure 5.16 shows the comparison between two techniques one is GA with K-means and another is GA with ANN for 600 elements. From the graph it is clear that the proposed approach carries out better results as compared to another approach. Also when the number of iterations escalate, the precision value falls. This might be due to the performance of the testing sample again and again, so that accurate value can be evaluated. The average value of GA-K- means is 95.56 and average value off GA-ANN is 96.71.

5.2.2.2 Recall for 600 Elements

Table 5.17 Recall for 600 Elements

Number of iterations	GA-K-means	GA-ANN
10	96.34	97.67
20	96.10	97.40
30	95.45	96.80
40	94.45	96.40
50	94.34	95.82
60	94.22	95.59

Figure 5.17 Recall for 600 Elements

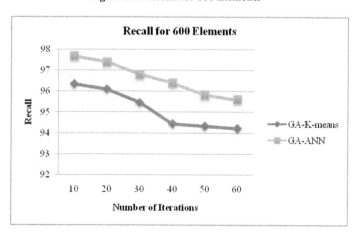

Figure 5.17 represents the comparison of recall using GA with ANN and K-means as a machine learning approach. From the graph it is clear that the said approach carries out better reults in contrast to another approach. At iteration 30th the value of GA-K-means is 95.45 and GA-ANN is 96.8. The average value of GA-K-means is 95.15 and GA-ANN is 96.61.

5.2.2.3 F-measure for 600 Elements

Table 5.18 F-measure for 600 Elements

Number of iterations	GA-K-means	GA-ANN
10	96.39	97.66
20	96.46	97.3
30	95.61	96.83
40	94.94	95.28
50	94.66	96.07
60	94.27	95.58

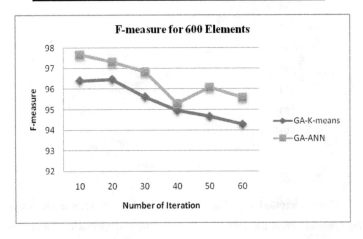

Figure 5.18 F-measure for 600 Elements

Figure 5.18 represents the comparison of F-measure using GA with ANN and K-means as a machine learning approach. In the graph, the blue and the orange lines are used to represents the F-measure values for GA with ANN and GA with the K-means approach, respectively At iteration 60th the value of GA-K-means is 94.27 and GA-ANN is 95.58. The mean worth of GA-K-means is 95.38 and mean worth of GA-ANN is 96.45.

5.2.3 Computed parameters for 800 elements

The desire of this work is to inspect the satisfaction level of workers in the company by considering different factors, as mentioned above. This segment describes the performance of the said work in terms of precision, recall, and F-measure for 800 Elements.

5.2.3.1 Precision for 800 Elements

Table 5.19 Precision for 800 Elements

Number of iterations	GA-K-means	GA-ANN
10	96.45	97.54
20	96.22	97.20
30	95.56	96.76
40	95.22	96.43
50	94.98	96.28
60	94.65	95.48

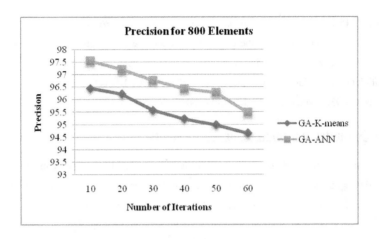

Figure 5.19 Precision for 800 Elements

Figure 5.19 shows the comparison between two techniques one is GA with K-means and another is GA with ANN for 800 elements. From the graph it is clear that the said approach Carries out better results in contrast to another approach. Also, when the number of iterations escalate , the precision value falls. This might be due to the performance of the testing sample again and again, so that accurate value can be evaluated. At iteration 60th the value of GA-K-means is 94.34 and value of GA-ANN is 965.56. The average value of GA-K-means is 95.56nd average value off GA-ANN is 96.71.

5.2.3.2 Recall for 800 Elements

Table 5.20 Recall for 800 Elements

Number of iterations	GA-K-means	GA-ANN
10	96.21	97.58
20	96	97.39
30	95.18	96.77
40	94.34	96.38
50	94.22	95.76
60	94.05	95.55

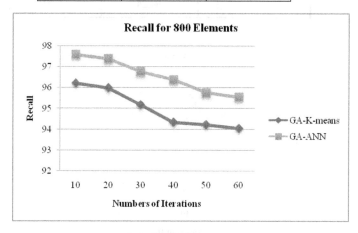

Figure 5.20 Recall for 800 Elements

Figure 5.20 represents the comparison of recall using GA with ANN and K-means as a machine learning approach. From the graph it is clear that the said approach carries out better results in contrast to another approach. In the graph, the red and the orange lines are used to represents the recall values for GA with ANN and GA with the K-means approach, respectively. From the graph, it has been examined that ANN performed well compared to the K-means approach with higher recall value. The average value of GA-K-means is 95 and GA-ANN is 96.57.

5.2.3.3 F-measure for 800 Elements

Table 5.21 F-measure for 800 Elements

Number of iterations	GA-K-means	GA-ANN
10	96.32	97.55
20	96.1	97.29
30	95.36	96.76
40	94.77	96.4
50	94.59	96.01
60	94.34	95.51

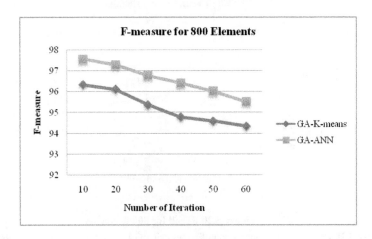

Figure 5.21 F-measure for 800 Elements

Figure 5.21 represents the comparison of F-measure using GA with ANN and K-means as a machine learning approach. In the graph, the blue and the orange lines are used to represents the F-measure values for GA with ANN and GA with the K-means approach, respectively At iteration 40and 50 the value of GA-K-means is 94.77, 94.59 and GA-ANN is 96.4, 96,01. The mean worth of GA-K-means is 95.24 and mean worth of GA-ANN is 96.58.

5.2.4 Computed Parameters for 1000 Elements.

The desire of this work is to inspect the satisfaction level of workers in the company by considering different factors, as mentioned above. This segment describes the performance of the said work in terms of precision, recall, and F-measure for 1000 Elements.

5.2.4.1 Precision for 1000 Elements

Table 5.22 Precision for 1000 Element

Number of iterations	GA-K-means	GA-ANN
10	96	97.49
20	96.10	97.17
30	95	96.66
40	94.88	96.40
50	94.67	96.22
60	94	95.43

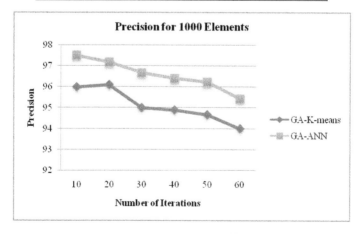

Figure 5.22 Precision for 1000 Elements

Figure 5.22 shows the comparison between two techniques one is GA with K-means and another is GA with ANN for 1000 elements. From the graph it is clear that the said approach carries out better results in contrast to another approach. Also, when the number of iterations escalate, the precision value falls. This might be due to the performance of the testing sample again and again, so that accurate value can be evaluated. The average value of GA-K-means is 95.51nd average value off GA-ANN is 96.61.

5.2.4.2 Recall for 1000 Elements

Table 5.23 Recall for 1000 Elements

Number of iterations	GA-K-means	GA-ANN
10	96	97.45
20	96.22	97.33
30	95	96.66
40	94.12	96.29
50	94.34	95.70
60	94	95.50

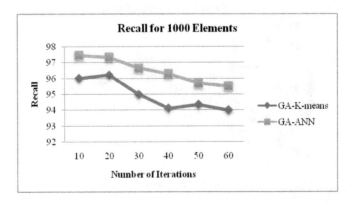

Figure 5.23 Recall for 1000 Elements

Figure 5.23 represents the comparison of recall using GA with ANN and K-means as a machine learning approach. In the graph, the blue and the orange lines are used to represents the recall values for GA with ANN and GA with the K-means approach, respectively. From the graph, it has been examined that ANN performed well compared to the K-means approach with higher recall value. The mean worth of GA-K-means is 94.94 and mean worth of GA-ANN is 96.48.

5.2.4.3 F-measure for 1000 Elements

Table 5.24 F-measure for 1000 Elements

Number of iterations	GA-K-means	GA-ANN
10	96	97.46
20	96.15	97.24
30	95	96.66
40	94.49	96.34
50	94.5	95.95
60	94	95.46

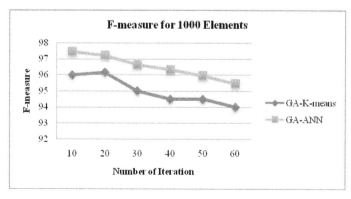

Figure 5.24 F-measure for 1000 Elements

Figure 5.24 represents the comparison of F-measure using GA with ANN and K-means as a machine learning approach. In the graph, the blue and the orange lines are used to represents the F-measure values for GA with ANN and GA with the K-means approach, respectively At iteration 10th and 60th the value of GA-K-means is 96, 94 and GA-ANN is 97.46, 95.46. The mean worth of GA-K-means is 95.03 and mean worth of GA-ANN is 96.51

CHAPTER 6 : CONCLUSION AND FUTURE SCOPE

Management of human capital is known as the most important asset of any enterprise. It's the combined sum of innate potential, expertise gained and mastery embodied by employee strengths consisting of managers, superiors, and rank judges. It is worth mentioning here that human capital must be used to the greatest extent to attain overall objectives. The output of the employee thus determines and eventually achieves the targets.

An automatic employee job satisfaction system has been proposed using an optimized neural network approach. The system will be of great significance in assisting HRs to solve problems related to job satisfaction levels. It provides an automatic data retrieval process so that timely decisions can be taken to enhance the performance or output of the company.

The proposed approach helps to save time by absolutely replacing the traditional manual component of background investigation that has been performed to evaluate employee's performance. The aim of this research is to design an automatic job performance analysis system using a machine learning approach.

The designed model has been well suited to examine the performance of employees in terms of precision, recall, and f-measure. Based on these factors, the satisfaction level predicted using three attributes passes as input data with multiple neurons in the hidden layer. The results show that the GA with the ANN prediction system has a better prediction effect with improved performance.

The improvement in precision, recall, and F- measure in the proposed work has been analyzed as 4.07 %, 2.05%, and 2.97 %, respectively, in contrast to the GA with the K-means approach.

6.1 FUTURE SCOPE

- Studies may be performed country specific. To obtain a broader view of this issue, companies who are not yet using AI but eager to utilize it in the future may be included in the research..

- Exit Interviews can be considered as one of the factors to improve work culture of an organization.

- Feedback of the employees can also be considered as input to determine Human Capital.

- A statistical method may be used to analyze how the choices made by AI with respect to hiring influenced the company's performance and sales numerically.

- Biases and discrimination occurs in recruitment have been discussed. It could therefore be examined in future if AI was able to eradicate gender gaps and prejudice amongst applicants for jobs.

REFERENCES

1. Anisimov, A.Y. & Obukhova, A.S. & Aleksakhina, Y.V. & Zhaglovskaya, A.V. & Kudra, A.A.. (2017). Strategic approach to forming a human resource management system in the organization. International Journal of Economic Perspectives. 11. 442-448.
2. Atteya, N. M. (2012). Testing the impact of the human resource management practices on job performance: An empirical study in the Egyptian joint venture petroleum companies. International Journal of Business and Social Science, 3(9).
3. Author: Soumyasanto Sen Soumyasanto Sen is an HR Technology, Author: & Soumyasanto Sen is an HR Technology. (2020, November 17). *AI and Automation in HR: Impact, Adoption and Future Workforce*. AIHR Digital. https://www.digitalhrtech.com/ai-in-hr-impact-adoption-automation/.
4. Amla, M., &Malhotra, P. M. (2017). Digital Transformation in HR. International Journal of Interdisciplinary and Multidisciplinary Studies (IJIMS), 4(3), 536-544.
5. Ayoub, K., & Payne, K. (2016). Strategy in the age of artificial intelligence. *Journal of strategic studies*, *39*(5-6), 793-819.
6. Ballal, I., Kavathekar, S., Janwe, S., Shete, P., &Bhirud, N. (2020). People Leaving the Job–An Approach for Prediction Using Machine Learning. IJRAR-International Journal of Research and Analytical Reviews (IJRAR), 7(1), 891-893.
7. Boselie, P., Dietz, G., & Boon, C. (2005). Commonalities and contradictions in HRM and performance research. *Human Resource Management Journal*, *15*(3), 67–94. https://doi.org/10.1111/j.1748-8583.2005.tb00154.x
8. Becker, B., & Gerhart, B. (1996). The Impact Of Human Resource Management On Organizational Performance: Progress And Prospects. *Academy of Management Journal*, *39*(4), 779–801. https://doi.org/10.2307/256712
9. Bebis, G., &Georgiopoulos, M. (1994). Feed-forward neural networks. *IEEE Potentials*, *13*(4), 27-31.
10. Berhil, S., Benlahmar, H., & Labani, N. (2020). A review paper on artificial intelligence at the service of human resources management. *Indonesian Journal of Electrical Engineering and Computer Science*, *18*(1), 32. https://doi.org/10.11591/ijeecs.v18.i1.pp32-40.
11. Boon, C., Hartog, D. N. D., & Lepak, D. P. (2019). A Systematic Review of Human Resource Management Systems and Their Measurement. *Journal of Management*, *45*(6), 2498–2537. https://doi.org/10.1177/0149206318818718.

12. Buchanan, B. G. (2005). A (Very) Brief History of Artificial Intelligence. *AI Magazine*, *26*(4), 53. https://doi.org/10.1609/aimag.v26i4.1848.
13. Cania, L. (2014). The impact of strategic human resource management on organizational performance. Economia. Seria Management, 17(2), 373-383.
14. Cooke, F. L., Schuler, R., &Varma, A. (2020). Human resource management research and practice in Asia: Past, present and future. *Human Resource Management Review*, 100778.
15. Coelho, F. D., Reis, R. Q., & de Souza, C. R. (2019). A genetic algorithm for human resource allocation in software projects. In *2019 XLV Latin American Computing Conference (CLEI)* (pp. 01-08). IEEE.
16. Cogin, J. A., Ng, J. L., & Lee, I. (2016). Controlling healthcare professionals: how human resource management influences job attitudes and operational efficiency. Human resources for health, 14(1), 55.
17. Čerka, P., Grigienė, J., & Sirbikytė, G. (2017). Is it possible to grant legal personality to artificial intelligence software systems? *Computer Law & Security Review*, *33*(5), 685–699. https://doi.org/10.1016/j.clsr.2017.03.022
18. Chaudhary, R. (2019). Green Human Resource Management and Employee Green Behavior: An Empirical Analysis. *Corporate Social Responsibility and Environmental Management*, *27*(2), 630–641. https://doi.org/10.1002/csr.1827.
19. Chams, N., & García-Blandón, J. (2019). On the importance of sustainable human resource management for the adoption of sustainable development goals. *Resources, Conservation and Recycling*, *141*, 109–122. https://doi.org/10.1016/j.resconrec.2018.10.006.
20. Kavya,D.S & Desai,D.(2016) "Comparative Analysis of K means Clustering Sequentially And Parallely" nature, Vol. 3, no. 4,.
21. Dhamija, P., Gupta, S., & Bag, S. (2019). Measuring of job satisfaction: the use of quality of work life factors. *Benchmarking: An International Journal*, *26*(3), 871–892. https://doi.org/10.1108/bij-06-2018-0155.
22. Davidescu, A. A., Apostu, S.-A., Paul, A., & Casuneanu, I. (2020). Work Flexibility, Job Satisfaction, and Job Performance among Romanian Employees—Implications for Sustainable Human Resource Management. *Sustainability*, *12*(15), 6086. https://doi.org/10.3390/su12156086
23. Delaney, J. T., & Huselid, M. A. (1996). The Impact Of Human Resource Management Practices On Perceptions Of Organizational Performance. *Academy of Management Journal*, *39*(4), 949–969. https://doi.org/10.2307/256718
24. Fernandes, E., Holanda, M., Victorino, M., Borges, V., Carvalho, R., & Erven, G. V. (2019). Educational data mining: Predictive analysis of academic performance of public school students in the capital of Brazil. *Journal of Business Research*, *94*, 335–343. https://doi.org/10.1016/j.jbusres.2018.02.012
25. Gabriel, A. S., Cheshin, A., Moran, C. M., & van Kleef, G. A. (2016). Enhancing emotional performance and customer service through human resources practices: A systems perspective. Human Resource Management Review, 26(1), 14-24.

26. Gupta, M. K., & Chandra, P. (2020). An empirical evaluation of K-means clustering algorithm using different distance/similarity metrics. In *Proceedings of ICETIT 2019* (pp. 884-892). Springer, Cham.

27. Gordini, N., &Veglio, V. (2017). Customers churn prediction and marketing retention strategies. An application of support vector machines based on the AUC parameter- selection technique in B2B e-commerce industry. Industrial Marketing Management, 62, 100-107

28. Ho, H., & Kuvaas, B. (2020). Human resource management systems, employee well-being, and firm performance from the mutual gains and critical perspectives: The well-being paradox. *Human Resource Management*, 59(3), 235–253. https://doi.org/10.1002/hrm.21990

29. Huang, W.-R., & Su, C.-H. (2016). The mediating role of job satisfaction in the relationship between job training satisfaction and turnover intentions. *Industrial and Commercial Training*, 48(1), 42–52. https://doi.org/10.1108/ict-04-2015-0029

30. HANDA, D. (2014). HUMAN RESOURCE (HR) ANALYTICS: EMERGING TREND IN HRM (HRM). *CLEAR International Journal of Research in Commerce & Management, 5*(6).

31. Islam, IshitaNafisa. "Human Resource Management Practices: Architects" Perception and Job Satisfaction." *Human Resource Management* 4, no. 1 (2016): 61.

32. Jain, P. K., Jain, M., &Pamula, R. (2020). Explaining and predicting employees' attrition:a machine learning approach. SN Applied Sciences, 2(4), 1-11.

33. Jawaad, M., Amir, A., Bashir, A., & Hasan, T. (2019). Human resource practices and organizational commitment: The mediating role of job satisfaction in emerging economy. *Cogent Business & Management, 6*(1), 1608668. https://doi.org/10.1080/23311975.2019.1608668.

34. Jain, S. (2017). IS ARTIFICIAL INTELLIGENCE –THE NEXT BIG THING IN HR ? International Conference on Innovation Research in Scinece, Techonology and Management (pp. 220-224). Rajasthan :ModiIntitute of Management & Technology.

35. Jeet, V., &Sayeeduzzafar, D. (2014). A study of HRM practices and its impact on employees job satisfaction in private sector banks: A case study of HDFC Bank. International Journal of Advance Research in Computer Science and Management Studies, 2(1).

36. Kramar, R. (2014). Beyond strategic human resource management: is sustainable human resource management the next approach?. The International Journal of Human Resource Management, 25(8), 1069-1089.

37. Kakulapati, V., Chaitanya, K. K., Chaitanya, K. V. G., &Akshay, P. (2020). Predictive analytics of HR-A machine learning approach. Journal of Statistics and Management Systems, 1-11.

38. Korff, J., Biemann, T., & Voelpel, S. C. (2016). Human resource management systems and work attitudes: The mediating role of future time perspective. *Journal of Organizational Behavior, 38*(1), 45–67. https://doi.org/10.1002/job.2110.

39. Kouziokas, G. N. (2017). The application of artificial intelligence in public administration for forecasting high crime risk transportation areas in urban environment. *Transportation Research Procedia, 24*, 467–473. https://doi.org/10.1016/j.trpro.2017.05.083

40. Ling, F. Y. Y., Ning, Y., Chang, Y. H., & Zhang, Z. (2018). Human resource management practices to improve project managers' job satisfaction. *Engineering, Construction and Architectural Management, 25*(5), 654–669. https://doi.org/10.1108/ecam-02-2017-0030

41. Longoni, A., Luzzini, D., &Guerci, M. (2018). Deploying environmental management across functions: the relationship between green human resource management and green supply chain management. *Journal of Business Ethics, 151*(4), 1081-1095.

42. Lloyd, S., Mohseni, M., &Rebentrost, P. (2013). Quantum algorithms for supervised and unsupervised machine learning. *arXiv preprint arXiv:1307.0411*.

43. Marler, J. H. (2012). Strategic human resource management in context: a historical and global perspective. *Academy of Management Perspectives, 26*(2), 6-11.

44. Mahmood, A., Akhtar, M. N., Talat, U., Shuai, C., & Hyatt, J. C. (2019). Specific HR practices and employee commitment: the mediating role of job satisfaction. *Employee Relations: The International Journal, 41*(3), 420–435. https://doi.org/10.1108/er-03-2018-0074.

45. Mishra, S. N., Lama, D. R., & Pal, Y. (2016). Human Resource Predictive Analytics (HRPA) for HR management in organizations. *International Journal of Scientific & Technology Research, 5*(5), 33-35.

46. Kumar, M., Husain, M., Upreti, N., & Gupta, D. (2010). Genetic Algorithm: Review and Application. *SSRN Electronic Journal*. https://doi.org/10.2139/ssrn.3529843

47. Noe, R. A., Hollenbeck, J. R., Gerhart, B. A., & Wright, P. M. (2007). Fundamentals of human resource management.

48. Nabi, M. N., Ahmed, A. A. T., & Rahman, M. S. (2017). *The Empirical Study on Human Resource Management Practices with Special Reference to Job Satisfaction and Employee Turnover at Investment Corporation of Bangladesh*. Human Resource Management Research. http://article.sapub.org/10.5923/j.hrmr.20170701.07.html.

49. Nunn, D. J. (2018, May 9). *Council Post: How AI Is Transforming HR Departments*. Forbes. https://www.forbes.com/sites/forbestechcouncil/2018/05/09/how-ai-is-transforming-hr-departments/?sh=287e6781c0f6.

50. Obedgiu, V. (2017). Human resource management, historical perspectives, evolution and professional development. *Journal of Management Development*.

51. Onyusheva, I. V., &Leskovskaya, E. B. (2017). Historical Background of Human Resource Management: Types and Theories. *Уральскийнаучныйвестник*, *2*(1), 021-028.
52. Otoo, F. N. K. (2019). Human resource management (HRM) practices and organizational performance. *Employee Relations: The International Journal*, *41*(5), 949–970. https://doi.org/10.1108/er-02-2018-0053
53. Paillé, P., Chen, Y., Boiral, O., & Jin, J. (2014). The impact of human resource management on environmental performance: An employee-level study. Journal of Business Ethics, 121(3), 451-466.
54. Pan, I., Nolan, L. B., Brown, R. R., Khan, R., van der Boor, P., Harris, D. G., &Ghani, R. (2017). Machine learning for social services: a study of prenatal case management in Illinois. *American journal of public health*, *107*(6), 938-944.
55. Malhotra, R., Singh, N., & Singh, Y. (2011). Genetic Algorithms: Concepts, Design for Optimization of Process Controllers. *Computer and Information Science*, *4*(2). https://doi.org/10.5539/cis.v4n2p39
56. Rajesh, D. S., Kandaswamy, M. U., &Rakesh, M. A. (2018). The impact of Artificial Intelligence in Talent Acquisition Lifecycle of organizations. International Journal of Engineering Development and Research, 6(2), 709-717.
57. Rani,S (2019)International Research journal of Management Sociology Humanities. https://doi.org/10.32804/irjmsh.
58. Dharwal, R. (2016). Applications of Artificial Neural Networks: A Review. *Indian Journal of Science and Technology*, *9*(1), 1–8. https://doi.org/10.17485/ijst/2016/v9i47/106807.
59. Rao, P., &Teegen, H. (2009). Human resource management.
60. Pagariya,R &Bartere (2013) ―Review Paper on Artificial Neural Networks‖ International Journal of Advanced Research in Computer Science, Vol. 4, no. 6, pp. 49-53
61. Roscoe, S., Subramanian, N., Jabbour, C. J., & Chong, T. (2019). Green human resource management and the enablers of green organisational culture: Enhancing a firm's environmental performance for sustainable development. *Business Strategy and the Environment*, *28*(5), 737–749. https://doi.org/10.1002/bse.2277
62. Sabuhari, R., Sudiro, A., Irawanto, D. W., & Rahayu, M. (2020). The effects of human resource flexibility, employee competency, organizational culture adaptation and job satisfaction on employee performance. *Management Science Letters*, 1777–1786. https://doi.org/10.5267/j.msl.2020.1.001
63. Sanger, T. D. (1989). Optimal unsupervised learning in a single-layer linear feedforward neural network. *Neural networks*, *2*(6), 459-473.
64. Saeed, B. B., Afsar, B., Hafeez, S., Khan, I., Tahir, M., & Afridi, M. A. (2018). Promoting employee's proenvironmental behavior through green human resource management practices. *Corporate Social Responsibility and Environmental Management*, *26*(2), 424–438. https://doi.org/10.1002/csr.1694
65. Sareen, D. (2018). "Relationship between strategic human resource management and job satisfaction." *International Journal of Current Research in Life Sciences* 7, no. 03: 1229-1233.

66. Shanmugam, A., & Kalyanaraman, N. (2019). An Analysis of Job Insecurity of Employees Working on I.T. & ITeS Companies, Resulting in Stress and Health Problems & their Perception towards the Career Growth —A Study with Reference to Chennai City. *Indian Journal of Public Health Research & Development*, *10*(8), 661. https://doi.org/10.5958/0976-5506.2019.01963.6

67. Siregar, E. I., &Hafnidar, S. (2020). THE MODEL OF EMPLOYEE SATISFACTION: A HUMAN RESOURCES MANAGEMENT PERSPECTIVE. *Journal of Accounting and Finance Management*, *1*(2), 125-141.

68. Silic, M., Marzi, G., Caputo, A., &Bal, P. M. (2020). The effects of a gamified human resource management system on job satisfaction and engagement. *Human Resource Management Journal*, *30*(2), 260-277

69. Selvarajan, T., Ramamoorthy, N., Flood, P. C., Guthrie, J. P., Maccurtain, S., & Liu, W. (2007). The role of human capital philosophy in promoting firm innovativeness and performance: test of a causal model. *The International Journal of Human Resource Management*, *18*(8), 1456–1470. https://doi.org/10.1080/09585190701502588

70. Stahl, G. K., Brewster, C. J., Collings, D. G., &Hajro, A. (2020). Enhancing the role of human resource management in corporate sustainability and social responsibility: A multi-stakeholder, multidimensional approach to HRM. *Human Resource Management Review*, *30*(3), 100708.

71. SUBASHINI, G. (2020). Artificial Intelligence in HRM. *Purakala with ISSN 0971-2143 is an UGC CARE Journal*, *31*(49), 56-62.

72. Taieb, S. B., & Hyndman, R. J. (2014). A gradient boosting approach to the Kaggle load forecasting competition. *International journal of forecasting*, *30*(2), 382-394

73. Tutar, H., &Sarkhanov, T. (2020). CHANGE FROM PERSONNEL MANAGEMENT TO HUMAN RESOURCE MANAGEMENT IS AN EPISTEMOLOGICAL NECESSITY OR RHETORIC CHANGE?. *Economic and Social Development: Book of Proceedings*, 306-313.

74. Truss, C. (2001). Complexities and Controversies in Linking HRM with Organizational Outcomes. *Journal of Management Studies*, *38*(8), 1121–1149. https://doi.org/10.1111/1467-6486.00275

75. Wirtz, B. W., Weyerer, J. C., & Geyer, C. (2019). Artificial intelligence and the public sector—applications and challenges. *International Journal of Public Administration*, *42*(7), 596-615.

76. Wang, C.-J. (2019). Linking Sustainable Human Resource Management in Hospitality: An Empirical Investigation of the Integrated Mediated Moderation Model. *Sustainability*, *11*(4), 1066. https://doi.org/10.3390/su11041066

77. Waterman, D., & Newell, A. (1971). Protocol analysis as a task for artificial intelligence. *Artificial Intelligence*, *2*(3-4), 285–318. https://doi.org/10.1016/0004-3702(71)90014-2

78. Yanli, Z., Shun, L., & Weibao, L. (2020). The Impact of Human Resource Management System on Enterprise Sustained Competitive Advantage in Competitive Strategy: The Mediating Role of Human Capital. *International Journal of Business and Social Science*, *11*(3). https://doi.org/10.30845/ijbss.v11n3a23

79. Yawalkar, M. V. V. (2019). a Study of Artificial Intelligence and its role in Human Resource Management. *International Journal of Research and Analytical Reviews (IJRAR)*, 20-24.
80. Yong, J. Y., Yusliza, M. Y., Ramayah, T., Jabbour, C. J. C., Sehnem, S., & Mani, V. (2019). Pathways towards sustainability in manufacturing organizations: Empirical evidence on the role of green human resource management. *Business Strategy and the Environment, 29*(1), 212–228. https://doi.org/10.1002/bse.2359
81. Zhao, X. (2008). A Study of Performance Evaluation of HRM: Based on Data Mining. *2008 International Seminar on Future Information Technology and Management Engineering.* https://doi.org/10.1109/fitme.2008.133

A

Thesis

On

DESIGN AND ANALYSIS OF HUMAN RESOURCES USING ARTIFICIAL INTELLIGENCE

By

Jaswinder Singh Sekhon

Regd. No. 2017300573

Under Guidance of

Dr. Harsh Sadawarti

Department of Computer Science

CT UNIVERSITY

LUDHIANA (PUNJAB)

INDIA

CHAPTER 6 : CONCLUSION AND FUTURE SCOPE

Management of human capital is known as the most important asset of any enterprise. It's the combined sum of innate potential, expertise gained and mastery embodied by employee strengths consisting of managers, superiors, and rank judges. It is worth mentioning here that human capital must be used to the greatest extent to attain overall objectives. The output of the employee thus determines and eventually achieves the targets.

An automatic employee job satisfaction system has been proposed using an optimized neural network approach. The system will be of great significance in assisting HRs to solve problems related to job satisfaction levels. It provides an automatic data retrieval process so that timely decisions can be taken to enhance the performance or output of the company.

The proposed approach helps to save time by absolutely replacing the traditional manual component of background investigation that has been performed to evaluate employee's performance. The aim of this research is to design an automatic job performance analysis system using a machine learning approach.

The designed model has been well suited to examine the performance of employees in terms of precision, recall, and f-measure. Based on these factors, the satisfaction level predicted using three attributes passes as input data with multiple neurons in the hidden layer. The results show that the GA with the ANN prediction system has a better prediction effect with improved performance.

The improvement in precision, recall, and F- measure in the proposed work has been analyzed as 4.07 %, 2.05%, and 2.97 %, respectively, in contrast to the GA with the K-means approach.

6.1 FUTURE SCOPE

- Studies may be performed country specific. To obtain a broader view of this issue, companies who are not yet using AI but eager to utilize it in the future may be included in the research..

- Exit Interviews can be considered as one of the factors to improve work culture of an organization.

- Feedback of the employees can also be considered as input to determine Human Capital.

- A statistical method may be used to analyze how the choices made by AI with respect to hiring influenced the company's performance and sales numerically.

- Biases and discrimination occurs in recruitment have been discussed. It could therefore be examined in future if AI was able to eradicate gender gaps and prejudice amongst applicants for jobs.

CPSIA information can be obtained
at www.ICGtesting.com
Printed in the USA
BVHW031533091222
653840BV00010B/1068